Unwins
Flowering Bulbs in Colour
for Garden, Home and Greenhouse

A practical guide by experts

Hamlyn
London · New York · Sydney · Toronto

First published in 1973 by
The Hamlyn Publishing Group Limited
Hamlyn House, Feltham,
Middlesex, England
in association with W. J. Unwin Ltd.,
Histon, Cambridge
Filmset in Great Britain by
V. Siviter Smith and Co. Ltd.,
Birmingham

Printed and bound in Great Britain by
Cox & Wyman Ltd., London, Fakenham
and Reading

ISBN 0 6003 1295 X

Foreword

For many years the bulbous kinds of flowers have, very deservedly, attracted the pens of horticultural writers and journalists. It is quite safe to say that much will still be written about them, for their popularity here and abroad increases ever more rapidly as the years go by.

Few could be better informed of the tastes and requirements of present-day amateur gardeners than the Directors of a firm like mine (W. J. Unwin Ltd., Histon, Cambridge). We felt certain that a new book on bulbous flowers—bulbs, corms, tubers and rhizomes— comprehensive, well illustrated and easily understood, would be generally welcomed.

In producing such a book we have been more than fortunate. Among our Directors and staff are competent writers and speakers with practical experience and a love of flowers. They fully understand the innumerable questions and problems which face not only the beginner but quite often the more knowledgeable amateur.

What my Directors had in mind was very clear: namely, a comprehensive book written in simple, easily-understood language, concise, yet omitting nothing of real importance. A book, indeed, which would enable anyone to make a choice of bulbs to suit his or her individual tastes, requirements and circumstances, giving sufficient cultural information to ensure satisfactory results to those with little or no gardening knowledge.

Even though this objective might appear somewhat ambitious and optimistic, I believe it has been well achieved. The book includes almost every kind of bulbous flower likely to be found in catalogues, shops, garden centres, nurseries or advertisements. Many of the subjects dealt with are beautifully illustrated in their natural colours, an invaluable guide when making one's choice. Though the reader may have no garden, greenhouse, frame or window-box, many beautiful flowers are indicated which can be grown easily and flowered quite successfully in any ordinary living room.

Admittedly the book was produced mainly to assist the beginner and those with little experience, but I feel sure that many who are much more experienced will enjoy it, as I have.

Chas. W. J. Unwin F.L.S.

The Publishers are grateful to
the following photographers
who provided the colour
transparencies and black and
white photographs for the
illustrations in this book:
Amateur Gardening
Pat Brindley
Robert Corbin
Ernest Crowson
Elsa Megson
Harry Smith
Dennis Woodland

Line drawings by Tony Streek

Contents

Chapter

Chapter 1 The value of bulbs

A bulb has been described as the neatest packaging job ever devised. Folded within the package, with miraculous skill and economy, are all the next season's leaves and right in the centre is the bud that will one day burst into a delightful flower. Warmth and moisture are needed to trigger off the natural growing process but planting bulbs is one way to become a successful gardener without worry or skill.

Although their actual formation is somewhat different, the same ease of culture is true of corms, tubers and rhizomes which, together with true bulbs, are usually referred to as 'bulbous plants'. Many gardeners are confused over the structural differences between bulbs and the other bulbous plants but they all have the same function. This is to tide the plant over adverse weather conditions such as drought or severe cold. They all store food, which enables rapid growth when placed under suitable conditions, and share the same life cycle. During growth and flowering, next year's flower is formed in miniature and food manufactured by the leaves is passed back to be stored in order to restart the cycle. After flowering the leaves and roots of that year's growth fade away to leave the swollen storage organ and the embryo flower and leaves of the next year.

With a little planning you can use a wide range of these bulbous plants to give a lovely display of flowers the whole year round and not only in spring and early summer as is frequently assumed.

By late February, snowdrops and crocuses emerge as the heralds of advancing spring and then, in an unbroken succession of bloom, come the delightful Kaufmanniana and brilliant Fosteriana tulips, the cheerful little muscari, the golden daffodils, blue scillas and gay chionodoxas. By mid-April, the fragrant hyacinths and Single and Double Early tulips are flowering bravely followed by the lovely

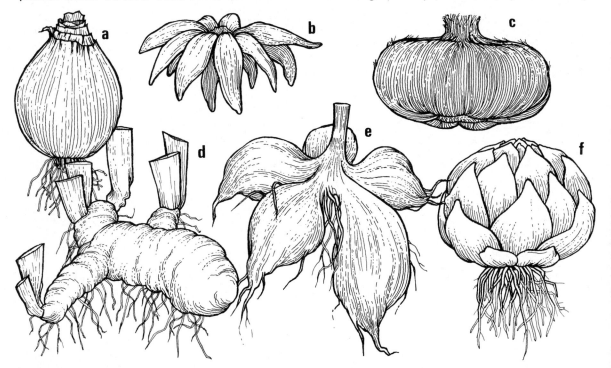

a Daffodil bulb **b** Ranunculus tubers **c** Gladiolus corm **d** Iris rhizome **e** Dahlia tubers **f** Lily bulb

Kaufmanniana tulips

Crinum powellii album

Mendel and Triumph tulips and red-cupped narcissi. Then come the full-flowered tulips of May, the graceful Cottage and Lily-flowered types and the stately Darwins in a multitude of colours.

You will get more fun and pleasure from your garden if you keep the scale of things in mind. Single Early tulips, for example, look particularly well in front of a low stone wall while the taller-growing Darwin and Cottage types are better sited in front of tall shrubs or against a high fence. Low-growing Kauf-mannianas will look lovely in a rock garden. Tulips may be grown in shady or wooded areas, as well as in sunny spots. Planted in partial shade they last at least ten days longer than when planted in the sun.

Muscari blend in almost anywhere and bluebells flower simultaneously with the longer-stemmed tulips. Hyacinths combine admirably with early tulips and small-cupped narcissi. When planted in groups in the borders, their beauty is enhanced if they are interplanted with white arabis, golden alyssum, aubrietas, double daisies and other spring bedding favourites.

Since daffodils can stand more shade than many other bulbs, their natural place in the garden is among shrubs, planted irregularly in grass or other less formal parts, or grouped at the back of the herbaceous border. Narcissi combine excellently with early tulips and hyacinths, while chionodoxa and muscari are also good companions.

Most gardeners would not be without gladioli, lilies and dahlias but few have explored the wide range of summer-flowering bulbs which provide rich colour with an abundance of flowers over a long period. They are easy to grow and are certain to bring pleasure and enjoyment.

There are many unusual and attractive forms to bring delight to every corner of the garden, from beds and borders to the rock garden. Stem heights range from under 12 in. to over 3 ft. with a colour range to vie with a rainbow. Below is a brief guide to summer garden pleasure with spring-planted bulbs.

If you want an autumn and early winter display in your garden you should plan a special summer bulb planting operation. Only a few kinds of bulbs are involved. These are: *Amaryllis belladonna*, colchicums, autumn crocus, hardy cyclamen and sternbergias. The rewarding results appear from September into December in the form of colourful, elegant flowers.

Type	Height	Colour	Flowering time
Acidanthera	2–3 ft.	White with maroon blotches	July–October
Anemone	1–1½ ft.	Wide range of rich colours	July–August
Brodiaea	6 in.–2 ft.	Wide range of colours	June–July
Crinum	2–4 ft.	White, purple, pink	August–September
Freesia	10–15 in.	Wide range of pastel colours	July–October
Galtonia	3–4 ft.	Milky white	July–August
Montbretia	1–2 ft.	Yellow, orange, copper, red	July–September
Ornithogalum	1½–2 ft.	White	July–September
Oxalis	8–12 in.	Carmine-red	July–September
Ranunculus	1–2 ft.	Wide range of lovely colours	June–August
Sparaxis	6–9 in.	Harlequin colours	June–August
Tigridia	1–2 ft.	Wide range of exotic colours	July–September

Dahlia Newchurch

Lilium regale

Colchicum agrippinum

Tigridias

9

Chapter 2 How to plant bulbs and their aftercare

In most gardens there can usually be found a place for a few bulbs and generally speaking most hardy bulbous plants flourish in any good well-drained soil, some even giving a creditable display under uncongenial conditions. Soil known as loam is ideal. This is a well-balanced mixture of clay, sand, humus material and lime. Where silver sand is available and a compost heap is constantly kept in being, it will be easy to add material which will render most soils suitable.

All soils will be improved by forking in peat and leafmould. Fresh manure, however, should not be used and an ideal site would be one that had been manured for a previous crop. Deep cultivation should be carried out well before planting time and a good dressing of bonemeal, at the rate of 2 oz. to the sq. yd., forked in to the soil during the final preparation, is very beneficial.

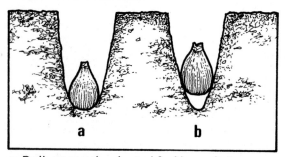

a Bulb correctly planted **b** Air pockets under the bulb may cause it to rot. This bulb has also been planted too high

A trowel is the handiest tool to use when planting. The bulb should be set firmly in position at the correct depth with the pointed end up. The soil should then be replaced making sure that the bulb has no air pocket underneath it as water might collect there causing the bulb and developing roots to rot. A bulb planting tool is available which is especially valuable when planting a quantity of naturalised bulbs. This will cut out a plug of soil or turf, leaving a clean round hole into which the bulb is placed. The plug can then be returned leaving little or no trace of having been removed.

As a general rule, spring-flowering bulbs can be planted at anytime during the autumn until frost hardens the ground. Daffodils are among the first to be planted from late August into October for they root early, but October and onwards is early enough for tulips and most other spring bulbs when the summer and autumn-flowering bedding plants have finished their displays.

Although all spring-flowering bulbs are hardy, in very cold areas some winter protection is desirable. Peat, branches of evergreens or dried bracken can be used but these should be removed during mild weather as soon as growth appears above the ground. Most spring-flowering bulbs, with the exception of tulips and hyacinths, may be left undisturbed for years for although the flowers may slightly decrease in size, the number of blooms will greatly increase.

Summer-flowering bulbs, with the exception of lilies, are not as hardy as those that flower in spring but they are just as easy to grow. Certain of them such as allium, Dutch iris, ixia, and ixiolirion bloom in June and July but must be planted in autumn. Stem-rooting lilies can be planted either in November or the spring. However, it is not too late to plan for a splendid display of bulbous flowers in your summer garden during March and April.

It is advisable to lift most summer-flowering bulbs in the autumn and store them away from the perils of frost for the winter. This is a minor effort to make in return for the

Lifting bulbous plants after they have flowered

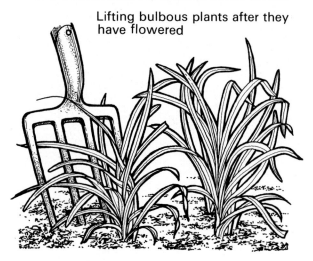

Heeling in the bulbs until the leaves die down

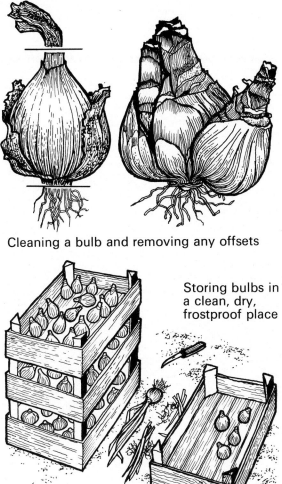

Cleaning a bulb and removing any offsets

Storing bulbs in a clean, dry, frostproof place

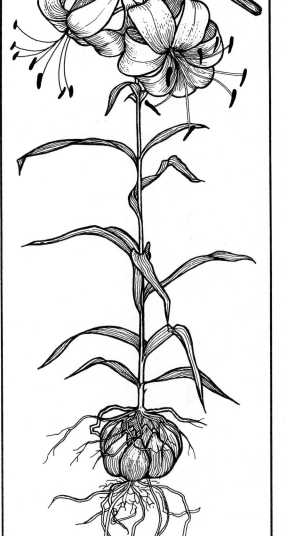

Stem-rooting lily

colourful show they create in your garden for months on end.

If it is necessary to lift any bulbous plants before the foliage has died down, do not leave them out of the ground but put them in the soil again in some out of the way place where the foliage may wither and die naturally, for it is the return of the sap from the leaves which helps to ripen the bulbs and complete the formation of the young flower buds for the next season. The leaves may be knotted together at this stage which will give the garden a neater appearance. Then you can finally lift them, remove loose skins and soil and store in a cool dry place until planting time comes round again.

Chapter 3   Colourful beds and borders

Beds and borders are inevitably focal points in any garden and to start the season with a gay and colourful effect, spring-flowering bulbs such as daffodils, hyacinths, tulips, crocuses and other smaller bulbs are un-paralleled.

Flower beds are basically formal and temporary. Bulbs and other plants are removed at the completion of the spring-flowering season and the spaces are then replanted with decorative summer-flowering subjects.

Borders, on the other hand, are usually completely informal and less stylised than bedding arrangements. While some may be replanted seasonally with fresh later-flowering stock, the majority of borders tend to be continuous displays of mixed subjects—shrubs, perennials, annuals, biennials and bulbs—to provide a longer succession of bloom without complete clearing and replanting.

Formal arrangements in beds and some borders, primarily those without shrubs and evergreens, can be most attractive and effective in enclosed gardens laid out geometrically and in association with architectural features. Informal arrangements are best limited to lawn beds, locations near pools and beside terraces, borders along walks, and against retaining walls.

Wherever possible avoid straight lines and formal squares. Plant in groups or clumps of three or more and if such spring-flowering bedding plants as wallflowers, forget-me-nots and polyanthus are also being used in the beds and borders, place the bulbs irregularly between the plants. Even when using only bulbs, plant so that each sort gradually merges into the next, rather than have severe demarcations.

Hyacinths and tulips are the chief formal bedding and border bulbs and they can be most spectacular when planted in blocks of a single colour or in patterned designs of various colours and shades. Narcissi and the taller irises can also be most effective when planted formally in beds and borders and so can Florist's or Poppy Anemones, but most miscellaneous bulbs like muscari, crocus, chionodoxas and scillas are of minor importance in this type of planting. Bulbs planted alone in beds and borders may be of one or more varieties, or more than one type of bulb may be used in a single bed, for example, bright blue muscari with golden daffodils.

As the mixtures become more complex, skill and taste must be carefully exercised to select types and varieties that will not only provide the desired colour combinations but will also flower at the same time.

Bulbs in formal beds can be used with other spring-flowering subjects for lovely effects. Pansies, violas, aubrieta, alyssum, forget-me-nots, polyanthus, primroses and wallflowers set out as ground cover beneath hyacinths, tulips and daffodils can be delightful. Hyacinths and pansies make a very attractive combination whether the colours harmonise or contrast, whereas forget-me-nots look splendid either with golden or white trumpet daffodils.

The gardener with a limited amount of space may not want to go in for the very latest varieties, especially when he is catering for cut flowers for the house. Some of the finest sorts for this purpose have been in cultivation for many years and continue to give good results.

Hyacinths in a bed set in paving

Bedding tulips

Mixed bulbs in an informal border

Chapter 4   Naturalising bulbs

Great interest and pleasure can be obtained from bulbs growing naturally in an informal manner. Although it is easier to produce a more effective display where considerable space is available, satisfactory results can be achieved where only a small area is involved. Patches of a few dozen bulbs will give a striking display as is often seen with bluebells under trees, hardy cyclamen around trees and shrubs, crocuses and anemones on grassy banks and the smaller-growing narcissi and tulips in shrubberies and in grassed-down orchards.

One advantage of growing bulbs in this way is that they can be left undisturbed for many years. Some gardeners split up the clumps every five or six years but this is not necessary as long as growth remains healthy. Possibly the size of the flowers may decrease but this is not usually important, especially since the actual number of blooms produced normally increases. The natural increase of bulbs planted in this way usually means that the shapes of the clumps vary, resulting in drifts of colour giving a magnificent display.

Bulbs to be naturalised should not be planted in rows or specially shaped groups. The usual method is to scatter the bulbs and plant them just where they fall. In this way a natural informal effect is secured.

Take a good look at your garden and you will surely find many more sites where you can provide colour and beauty. While naturalised bulbs require a minimum of care, do treat them as valued permanent residents of the garden. It is essential that the soil they are planted in is deep, fertile and well drained. Bulbs must be planted at the correct depths, using a spade, trowel or bulb planter.

When planting in lawns, lift sections of the turf, work over the soil, mix in a little humus and also some bonemeal at the rate of 2 oz. to the sq. yd., then scatter the bulbs on top and plant before replacing the turf. If you use a bulb planter, make sure the soil is loose and in firm contact all round the bulbs.

All naturalised bulbs will benefit from an annual application of bonemeal or complete fertiliser at the rate of 2 oz. per sq. yd. Those naturalised in grassy places under trees and shrubs can be helped by an application of peat or leafmould while they are dormant.

Naturalised bulbs will go on for years, multiplying and creating new garden pictures. If, after a number of years, they do become overcrowded, lift the bulbs after the foliage has died down, separate, sort for size and store the bigger bulbs for replanting at the appropriate time.

Many bulbs grow quite happily in grass such as banks and slopes, rough areas and woodland glades, but do not plant them in a lawn which has to be mown. The following season's flowers depend on the foliage being allowed to die down naturally and if the leaves are cut off while still green, the growing and flowering cycle will be interrupted.

Where possible there is much to be said for naturalising particular bulbs to fit in with the surroundings. For instance yellow daffodils look well growing near the white-stemmed birches. Crocuses in white, yellow, blue or striped create attention when growing in quantity in the orchard, at approaches to woodlands and under large trees.

When naturalising bulbs in dozens rather than hundreds, it is wise to relate them closely to an important shrub, tree or evergreen. Place bright yellow Winter Aconites beneath the winter-bronzed foliage of a mahonia, or snowdrops can be scattered in groups in the shelter of evergreen shrubs. Use blue muscari under gay yellow forsythias or around chaenomeles. Colonies of blue or white chionodoxas are most effective near azaleas or beneath magnolias. Carpet the ground under *Viburnum fragrans* or cotoneasters with the lovely blue *Scilla sibirica* or the white form *alba*.

Combine your naturalised daffodils with pastel grey-blue *Puschkinia libanotica*, *Muscari armeniacum*, or *Chionodoxa luciliae*, or naturalise them under flowering cherries, dogwoods and light-foliaged trees of all kinds. If you have a rather moist and partially shaded area try naturalising camassias there. Their bright blue flowers do well in grass and at approaches to woodlands. The common bluebell, *Scilla nutans*, multiplies rapidly when naturalised in woody areas. Colonies of *Fritillaria meleagris*, with their mottled flowers, look delightful under the spreading branches of cotoneasters or in grass.

The pink, blue and white blooms of *Anemone blanda* or the blue flowers of *A.*

A bulb planting tool with an enlarged drawing to show a plug of soil removed and the positioning of the bulb in the hole

Naturalised bulbs being planted with a trowel under a tree

Daffodils naturalised under a tree

Crocuses naturalised in grass

apennina produce endless colour in partially shaded positions. *Chionodoxa sardensis* is the first really blue flower of the year.

Generally speaking, tulips are not suitable for naturalisation but some of the species tulips do very well when planted in this way. The rose-red and creamy-white *Tulipa clusiana* looks lovely naturalised under flowering trees such as cherry and crataegus. The whole group of Kaufmanniana hybrid tulips in a wide range of bright colours will naturalise effectively. Colonies of the lovely little *T. tarda* planted in sunny positions look superb.

Valuable for massing and naturalising are the Spring Snowflakes, *Leucojum vernum*, producing little white bells tipped with green from early February onwards. Dwarf ornithogalums can be planted at random in shady positions near shrubs and hedges and naturalised in places where few other bulbs will flourish. *Ornithogalum nutans* bears silvery-grey and pale green flowers on 9-in. stems in March whilst *O. umbellatum*, the Star of Bethlehem, yields delightful white flowers on 10-in. stems in May.

Erythroniums in white, yellow or with pink or purple markings look well in sheltered areas. A few lilies can be naturalised. Try some of the lovely Mid Century group in grass in the wild garden where they can catch the morning sun. They flower in June–July. The August-flowering *Lilium tigrinum* will flower profusely year after year when naturalised.

Autumn-flowering crocuses can be naturalised in the rock garden and colchicums, if planted in grass under tall trees in dry exposed parts of the garden, will flower profusely each year. The yellow crocus-like flowers of *Sternbergia lutea* are very effective on grassy banks and slopes and once established bring colour to the October garden.

Hardy cyclamen are most easily grown and will thrive in shady positions under trees or on a hedge bank. Plant from July onwards covering the corms with 2 to 3 in. of soil. Among the best species is *Cyclamen neapolitanum* with rose-pink flowers appearing in autumn before the silvery-mottled foliage develops. *C. europaeum* also produces its sweetly scented carmine-rose flowers in autumn. *C. repandum* blooms in April and May, its crimson flowers being well set off by the handsome mottled foliage.

Cyclamen neapolitanum and autumn crocuses

Fritillaria meleagris

17

Chapter 5   Bulbs for the rock garden

Rock and alpine gardens are often made in odd corners as well as in more prominent situations. Wherever they may be placed, in sunshine or shade, there are showy bulbous subjects which can be used to give a lovely display. Plantings should be quite informal in character and this is the main reason why the smaller growing or miniature bulbs are so suited for cultivation in the rock garden and they can be chosen to produce colour at different times of the year.

After you have made your selection of the better known and more conventional subjects, look for some of the less common and choose some with which you may not be familiar. These are often found under the heading 'miscellaneous' in the majority of catalogues. Most have no special cultural needs and you will be pleasantly surprised by the delightful display you will secure.

In a well-made rock garden, there are crevices and interstices where little groups of three or more can be planted. They usually increase to give a bold display after a year or two. While it is true that muscari and a few other bulbs can be placed so that they penetrate a carpet of growth from perennial rock plants, only a few are successful under such conditions. Most, particularly the choicer kinds, are happy where they are unhampered and where the ground is clear around them so that their foliage can mature properly and the bulbs obtain the ripening they need. Although colchicums are suitable for selected positions in the rock garden, they should be placed with care for their foliage may block out or even smother nearby smaller plants which develop later.

If the soil is on the heavy side or water from surrounding ground is liable to drain on to the site, it is advisable to plant on slightly raised beds and mounds. In fact, this treatment is advisable for subjects that die down in the early summer so that they can dry off for a short period.

Apart from their value for giving a display in the front of the border or for naturalising, the following are ideal for the rock garden whatever its size.

Anemone blanda has beautiful star-shaped flowers in blue, pink, mauve or white which brighten the rock garden in March and April, as do the lavender-blue, daisy-like flowers of *A. apennina. A. fulgens,* which yields scarlet flowers in April—May, and St Bavo, with lovely pastel blooms at the same time, are also suitable in sun or partial shade. Plant all these in early autumn about 2 in. deep and 4 in. apart. Wait until March or April to plant the large-flowered de Caen and St Brigid anemones which come in many brilliant shades of red, purple, mauve, rose and white.

Chionodoxas, Glory of the Snow, should be planted in September or October 2 to 3 in. deep and 1 to 2 in. apart. They bloom as early as February continuing into April and grow about 6 in. high. *Chionodoxa gigantea* has light blue flowers with a white centre; *C. luciliae* is lilac blue with a pale star-shaped centre while *C. sardensis* is bright blue.

Crocus species will provide a continuous show from January onwards. *Crocus chrysanthus* has many varieties in white, primrose, canary yellow, golden and bronze shades as well as pastel blue. *C. susianus*, the Cloth of Gold crocus with bright yellow-orange flowers, appears by mid-February. *C. tomasinianus* is silvery lilac. By the end of February the pale greyish-lavender buds of *C. sieberi* open to reveal a pure lilac interior with golden-orange throat. The large-flowering Dutch hybrids show colour from March. Plant all these crocuses in September or October placing the corms 3 to 4 in. deep.

The Winter Aconites break through the ground early in January providing a cheerful show with their buttercup-yellow flowers. Plant the tiny tubers in autumn 2 in. deep and 2 to 3 in. apart. *Eranthis hyemalis*, golden yellow, is the earliest to bloom. *E. cilicica*, with deeper yellow blooms, bursts forth a little later as do the much larger golden-yellow blooms of *E. tubergeniana.*

The Snake's Head Fritillary or *Fritillaria meleagris* is so called because its nodding, bell-shaped flowers, carried on slender foot-high stems, are spotted and chequered rather like the skin of a snake. They are in shades of purple and white and are produced in April and May. They should be planted in autumn in cool positions about 3 in. deep.

Snowdrops have frosty-white, bell-like flowers as early as January. Plant in autumn about 4 in. deep and 2 to 3 in. apart in moist

Crocuses and snowdrops in a rock garden

Erythronium dens-canis

humus-filled soil in light shade. In addition to the common snowdrop, *Galanthus nivalis*, try the double-flowering form, *G. nivalis flore-pleno*.

There are a number of the dwarf species of iris which flower from January to March. They include the sweetly scented *Iris bakeriana*, lavender blue; *I. danfordiae*, lemon yellow; *I. histrioides major*, blue; and *I. reticulata*, violet, which has several sweetly scented forms. All grow from 3 to 9 in. tall and are long lasting. Plant them in the autumn about 4 in. deep in semi-shaded positions where their rich colourings are more pronounced and their flowering period is lengthened.

Leucojum vernum, the Spring Snowflake, sends up white flowers tipped green on 6-in. stems, looking rather like a choice snowdrop.

The lovely little *Puschkinia libanotica* has silvery-blue flowers with deep blue stripes in late March and April.

Grape Hyacinths brighten the rock garden from February onwards. Chief among the species are *Muscari armeniacum*, in bright shades of blue, and the unique *M. plumosum* or Feather Hyacinth which has large heads of plume-like violet flowers in May. Plant muscari in autumn 3 in. deep and 2 to 3 in. apart.

Erythronium dens-canis, the Dog's Tooth Violet, produces flowers in lovely delicate

Chionodoxa luciliae

Anemone blanda

Narcissus nanus

shades of white, pink, rose and purple in March and April. Its marbled foliage is attractive even after flowering time is over. Purchase mixed hybrids or named varieties and plant in autumn in peat-rich soil in somewhat moist shadowed places in the rock garden or border. Plant erythroniums in groups, placing the bulbs at least 6 in. deep.

Ornithogalum umbellatum, Star of Bethlehem, produces white blooms shaded green on 10 to 12-in. stems in May. Plant in autumn about 4 in. deep and 3 to 5 in. apart.

Scillas like positions that are open and sunny in the winter. Flowering from February onwards, *Scilla tubergeniana* produces silvery-blue flowers on 4-in. stems; *S. bifolia* is 5 in. tall and sky blue shading to pale blue, and its variety *rosea* is pink. *S. sibirica* produces cobalt-blue flowers on 4-in. stems in March and April, while the variety Spring Beauty has bright blue flowers on 6-in. stems. There is also a lovely white form.

The dwarf narcissi are ideal for rock gardens for they mingle well with creeping plants such as aubrieta, campanulas and raoulia. The tiniest of all is *Narcissus minimus*, a really delightful variety with golden flowers appearing in February and March on 2 to 3-in. stems. The varieties of *N. bulbocodium* are both quaint and attractive. The form known as

conspicuus is often referred to as the Yellow Hoop Petticoat, while there is also a white variety, both growing 6 in. high. The Cyclamineus varieties produce exquisitely formed, long lasting little trumpets and they are available in separate shades of yellow. *N. triandrus albus* is the Angel's Tears Daffodil producing on 7-in. stems clusters of elegant creamy-white flowers in March. *N. nanus* has a clear yellow trumpet and grows 4 in. tall. There are many forms varying in height from 8 to 12 in. Whichever of these dwarfs you plant you will be delighted with the display and the interest they provide.

Oxalis adenophylla is one of the best of this large family producing pretty dainty lilac-pink flowers throughout the summer. It forms a compact rosette of silvery leaves.

Sparaxis like sunny well-drained positions where they will produce their richly coloured flowers on 6 to 9-in. stems. Particularly good is the variety Fire King with its flaming red blooms.

Triteleia, sometimes known as milla and classed now as brodiaea, produces its starry sweet-scented bluish-white flowers in May on stems 4 to 6 in. high.

Chapter 6 Bulbs for window-boxes and other ornamental containers

With care it is possible to have colour in window-boxes and other ornamental containers throughout the year but this does require some thoughtful planning. You must ensure that there are no colour clashes although suitable contrasts in colour and habit add to the interest and effect.

Planning a window-box display is equally as important as planning a garden. Almost any plants, from dwarf evergreens and shrubs to bedding plants and seeds, will flourish in a well-tended window-box but the size of the plants should be related both to the size of the box and the surroundings.

Where there are permanent occupants in the window-box, there is usually sufficient space to allow a few other subjects to be planted and it is therefore advisable to put in something which will prove colourful, not only during spring and summer, but for other

Prince of Austria—a Single Early tulip

times too. Alternatively, where the boxes are cleared several times a year, some thought must be given as to the plants needed to provide a continuous display. This is easier where inner movable boxes are used, for certain plants can be started into growth while the earlier display is finishing.

As in the garden, autumn and spring are the chief planting months. However, you can have a few plants growing in pots at any time of the year ready for replacing items which may die or otherwise prove unsuitable for window-box culture.

Bulbs are the window-box gardener's best investment and it is not without good reason that they are so widely grown and depended upon. They are hardy and rewarding, thriving with the minimum of attention and producing colour freely whether in full sun or partial shade. There are bulbs to provide a show virtually round the year and the various types and varieties not only complement each other but they can be interplanted freely with other plants.

The greatest variety is found in spring-flowering subjects which are planted the previous autumn. It pays to buy good quality bulbs for the embryo flower is, or should be, already in the bulb when you buy it. A little extra leafmould or peat and silver sand will help to provide ideal growing conditions, but never allow bulbs to come into direct contact with manure. A trowel is the best tool for planting. Holes made with any other form of pointed implement are not always completely filled in which results in an air pocket at the base of the bulb.

The following is a list of bulbs suitable for growing in window-boxes but it is by no means comprehensive. Reference to catalogues will reveal an almost unbelievably wide range of bulbs of varying colours, heights and habit. For boxes at windows and on balconies, it is advisable to choose the shorter growing bulbs as winds can play havoc with tall stemmed plants and staking in boxes is not particularly attractive. Nevertheless there is a wide choice and type of bulb and scores upon scores of varieties that will yield big dividends in colour and pleasure.

The list includes: aconites; *Anemone blanda; Chionodoxa luciliae* and *C. sardensis;*

Daffodils in a lead tank

Double tulips and primulas in a window-box

Narcissus Edward Buxton and *Tulipa fosteriana* Madame Lefeber

the winter, spring and autumn-flowering crocuses; *Erythronium dens-canis*; *Fritillaria meleagris*; snowdrops both single and double flowered; dwarf iris including *danfordiae*, *histrioides major*, *reticulata* and its named hybrids; and muscari.

There are many dwarf narcissi which are ideal for window-boxes and balcony boxes including *bulbocodium conspicuus*; *cyclamineus* and its varieties; the tiny *minimus*; *triandrus albus* or Angel's Tears, and the sturdy short-stemmed *triandrus* varieties like Moonshine and Silver Chimes and that outstanding miniature trumpet daffodil, W. P. Milner. Jonquils too always create interest.

Hyacinths are simply superb for window-box cultivation. Scillas do particularly well in boxes, including *bifolia*, *sibirica* Spring Beauty and *tubergeniana* for early flowering and the taller *campanulata* for later flowering.

The brilliantly coloured species tulips provide a wide choice, including *clusiana*, *eichleri*, *persica*, *praestans*, *tarda*, the lily-flowered *kaufmanniana* and short-stemmed *greigii* varieties, many with attractively coloured leaves. The Single Early and Double Early tulips are available in many varieties. For later flowering, choose the Double Late or Peony-flowered varieties. The stems are taller but they look superb towards the back of boxes.

With tubs, urns and other larger receptacles on terraces, steps, paved areas or other focal points in the garden, one does not have to be concerned with the height factor. In these containers narcissi ranging from the golden and the white Trumpets to the Large and Small-cupped, the Doubles, the Jonquils and Poeticus are all ideal.

All the bulbs mentioned as suitable for window and balcony-boxes will do well in urns, tubs and larger receptacles, either on their own or combined with selections of plants. Hyacinths freely planted in bigger receptacles will produce a long lasting show in a host of colour schemes.

Apricot Beauty—a Mendel tulip

Mixed bulbs in a trough

Chapter 7   An A-Z guide to hardy bulbous plants

Acidanthera
Natives of Ethiopia, acidantheras have adapted themselves admirably to our climate and have proved to be strong and rapid growers. From late July into October, *Acidanthera bicolor murielae* produces a succession of large white fragrant flowers with maroon blotches at their centres. Five or six flowers usually open at one time on each 2 to 3-ft. stem. The foliage resembles that of gladioli and for this reason they were once thought to be scented gladioli. They are superb for cutting and will last a long time especially when picked in bud.

For the best results the corms should be planted in mid-May about 3 in. deep and about 6 in. apart. They prefer a position in full sun and to be sheltered from the wind. They are resistant to rain and are particularly charming in a bed of mixed summer bulbs or in a south-facing border. They like a light well-drained soil and appreciate the addition of leafmould or thoroughly decomposed manure.

Agapanthus
These are sometimes known as Lilies of the Nile or African Lilies. They have graceful foliage with large handsome funnel-shaped flowers. In very mild districts the plants thrive out of doors in warm sunny positions and a sandy loam although they are really only half hardy and are therefore more suitable for growing in pots for the conservatory and cool greenhouse. They may then be kept out of doors during the summer months.

When grown in tubs or pots, agapanthus like a compost of good loam, leafmould, decayed manure and silver sand. The best time for planting is early March and the thick fleshy rhizomes can be placed singly in a 9 or 10-in. pot or several in a larger receptacle. They may remain undisturbed for many years. When necessary the clumps should be divided in the spring and normally the divisions soon become established. Plenty of water is needed in summer and a few applications of liquid manure will prove beneficial.

Agapanthus umbellatus, the best-known species, produces stout stems 2 to 3 ft. high, surmounted by an umbel of bright blue flowers. Its strap-shaped leaves, sometimes up to 2½ ft. long, are freely produced. There is

also a fine white form as well as a double rich blue.

The Headbourne Hybrids are of complex parentage and have been developed in recent years. They are hardier than the species and the colours range from pale blue to deep violet blue.

Allium
The ornamental alliums vary greatly in size from some which are only a few inches high to others which are several feet. Many different colours are available varying from pure white to deep purple. All produce ball-shaped flower heads freely from May to July, some being solid, others tasselled. They thrive almost anywhere. The taller species are very showy in borders and shrubberies, the smaller growing ones being ideal for the rock garden or front of the border. Some can be used in long lasting flower arrangements and none of them will give off their onion smell unless bruised.

Plant the bulbs in the autumn, covering them with two to three times their own depth with soil. The smaller growing species can be planted 2 to 3 in. apart, the larger ones 8 to 9 in.

Among the best species is *Allium aflatunense*, the Powder Puff, which produces dense rounded heads of lilac-purple flowers on 2 to 3-ft. stems. *A. albopilosum*, sometimes known as the Butterflies' Haven, has heads of starry lilac flowers which are as much as 10 to 12 in. across on 2-ft. stems. *A. caeruleum*, 2 ft., produces globular heads of cornflower blue. *A. moly* is an old garden favourite with bluish-green leaves. Sometimes known as the Golden Garlic, it has umbels of yellow flowers on 10 to 12-in. stems. *A. neapolitanum*, which is 15 in. high, produces heads of sweetly scented white flowers. This species can also be forced. *A. ostrowskianum* has carmine-pink flowers on 6-in. stems making it ideal for the rock garden.

Alstroemeria
Often known as Peruvian Lilies, these tuberous-rooted perennials are very elegant. From June onwards the leafy stems, which are from 1 to 4 ft. high, bear umbels of richly coloured funnel-shaped flowers.

Acidanthera

Agapanthus

Allium albopilosum

Amaryllis belladonna

27

Alstroemeria

St Brigid anemones

They prefer a sheltered well-drained position and planting is best done in April. If established plants are given an annual mulching of well-decayed manure in the spring this will not only supply nourishment but will also give some protection from frost damage.

Excellent as cut flowers, there are many species and varieties including *Alstroemeria aurantiaca lutea*, yellow spotted carmine; *A. pelegrina*, clear pink; and *A. haemantha*, blood red. There are several named orange forms and the hybrids of *A. ligtu* are exceptional in that they provide exquisite shades of pink, orange, yellow and carmine.

Amaryllis
Amaryllis belladonna, known in this country for over two hundred years as the Belladonna Lily, is a native of South Africa. It is one of the most charming of autumn-flowering bulbs, blooming freely when established. Each stout stem, 15 to 18 in. high, carries at its top from six to ten funnel-shaped flowers which are a delightful shade of soft rose and sweetly fragrant. There are several forms although one rarely finds more than the type offered in catalogues.

A dry sunny bank or the foot of a south wall will form an ideal site for the Belladonna Lily for it likes shelter from severe frosts and cold winds and a well-drained soil. If the bulbs are planted in August or early September, they will bloom within a few weeks. They should be set on a little silver sand and covered with not less than 4 to 5 in. of good loamy soil.

Leave the bulbs undisturbed for some years and they will flower freely each autumn, especially if in very severe winters a little straw or bracken is placed over them. The dull green, strap-shaped leaves are produced in spring after the flowers have died and remain until late summer.

Anemone
Among the many species of anemone in cultivation none is more easy to grow than the hardy *Anemone nemorosa*, often called the Wood Anemone and a native of the British Isles. While they are quite happy at the front of the ordinary flower border or rock garden, they are really seen at their best growing on grassy slopes and banks, preferably where some shade is afforded during the day. Even the finely cut, hairy leaves are ornamental and the rose-tinged white flowers, growing on 5 to 6-in. stems, are often 1½ in. in diameter. They make a really bright show during April and May. There are several admirable varieties including *alba major*, large white; *alleni*, soft

Allium moly

Brodiaea uniflora

lavender blue; Royal Blue, rich lavender blue; and *robinsoniana*, with silvery-lavender flowers and prominent yellow anthers.

The Poppy Anemone, *A. coronaria*, has varieties with showy flowers in shades of pink, red and blue in spring and early summer. Two excellent strains—the St Brigid and de Caen have been bred from it.

The St Brigid anemones are of very graceful habit with large semi-double flowers all showing a blue-black central base. Greatly prized for cutting, they grow 10 in. high and the mixture contains many good hues. The de Caen anemones have large single flowers in mainly red and blue shades and also make splendid cut flowers.

Anemone nemorosa should be planted 2 in. deep in a rather leafy or peaty soil in September or October. *A. coronaria* and its strains should be given a good, fairly rich, well-drained soil in a sheltered sunny place and be planted from October to April to achieve a succession of flowers. The tubers should be soaked for a few hours before they are planted 2 in. deep and 4 in. apart. Early plantings should be protected in winter with a scattering of peat or chopped straw. The tubers should either be lifted when the foliage dies down in the summer and stored or left undisturbed and protected during the winter.

Brodiaea

Catalogued at various times as triteleias and millas but now definitely classed as brodiaeas, all varieties flower in June and July and do best in a well-drained soil in full sun. They are admirable subjects for the rock garden or front of the border.

Brodiaea coccinea (*B. ida-maia*), sometimes known as the Californian Fire Cracker, has 15-in. stems and beautiful green-tipped, crimson flowers. *B. congesta*, 12 in., has small bluish-lilac heads. *B. uniflora*, well known under the name *Milla uniflora*, is among the most popular of all. Growing about 6 in. tall, it has flowers which remain in bloom for a long time. Down the centre of each pale lavender petal runs a thin violet stripe and the freely produced fragrant flowers almost hide the grassy foliage.

Camassia

These are bulbs which will thrive almost anywhere, in sun or partial shade and in any well-drained soil. During July and August they bear a profusion of starry flowers and produce a delightful effect when planted in quantity in herbaceous borders, the rock garden, in odd corners or in a special plot reserved for cutting. No special culture is needed and they grow vigorously, increasing well if left undisturbed for several years. To keep the bulbs in good condition, the clumps should be lifted and divided every third year. Plant 4 in. deep and allow at least 3 in. between the bulbs.

Camassia cusickii has pale lavender-blue star-shaped flowers on 2-ft. stems and forms a rosette of glaucous-green foliage. *C. esculenta* has graceful 18-in. spikes of rich blue flowers while *C. leichtlinii* is a striking brilliant blue on 3-ft. stems.

Chionodoxa

Closely related to both scillas and hyacinths, the chionodoxas are natives of the mountainous regions of Asia Minor. They are perfectly hardy and are amongst the earliest of lovely spring-flowering bulbous subjects.

Planting can be carried out in October, burying the bulbs 2 in. deep in any good, well-drained soil. They are also excellent in pots or pans.

The following species, all growing 6 or 7 in. high, can be depended upon to give a good show. *Chionodoxa luciliae*, clear sky blue with white centre; *C. gigantea*, large clear blue flowers with small white centre, and its variety *alba*, pure white. *C. sardensis* is one of the very brightest and best of all, with rich gentian-blue flowers produced in little sprays.

Colchicum

Colchicums are handsome autumn-flowering bulbs which are often wrongly called autumn crocus because of their large crocus-like blooms in white and every shade of pink, mauve and purple. They are not, however, related to the true crocus. They are sometimes known as Meadow Saffrons and many gardeners call them Naked Ladies because they are quite devoid of foliage at flowering time in the autumn and only produce their broad, lush foliage later in the spring.

Colchicum flowers are 6 to 8 in. high but the prolific and decorative foliage that appears in the spring is often as tall as 15 to 18 in. This means they should not be planted where their foliage interferes with spring-flowering subjects such as near dwarf alpines, at the edge of borders, or in front of the rock garden. The best place to plant them is in grass under tall trees, in dry, exposed parts of the garden, around and under shrubs, at the fringe of woodlands, or in wild gardens. However, they should not be planted where cattle graze as the foliage is poisonous. Carefully sited in groups of four or more they are attractive in borders and in the rock garden where they produce flowers profusely every year.

Colchicums are easy to grow, thriving in well-drained soil and in full sun or partial shade. Despite the size of the irregularly shaped corms they need only a 2 or 3-in. covering of soil. The gorgeous flowers spring from each corm shortly after planting in late July or August while the foliage that emerges in spring grows on until summer. When the leaves die down, the corms can be lifted, the clusters separated, and the corms replanted. This is only necessary, however, when the clumps become overcrowded, about once every four or five years.

Colchicum autumnale is the best known species and several varieties are well worth planting. *C. autumnale major* (Byzantinum) produces a profusion of soft lilac-mauve flowers which are 6 in. tall in September and October. This variety can also be grown dry in the house by placing the corm on a saucer, without soil or water. *C. autumnale minor*, also 6 in. tall, blooms later with smaller but abundant rose-lilac, almost star-shaped flowers.

Colchicum speciosum has large deep purple flowers of erect habit on 8-in. stems in October and November. *C. agrippinum*, sometimes known as *C. tessellatum*, has very pretty flowers which are tessellated or chequered rosy purple and lilac white.

Large-flowered colchicum hybrids blooming from September to November include: Autumn Queen, purple-violet, large cup-shaped flowers; The Giant, large rosy-lilac flowers with white base, most vigorous; Violet Queen, large deep mauve flowers with white stripe; Lilac Wonder, pinkish-violet flowers with white stripe; and Waterlily, enormous lilac-mauve double flowers on sturdy stems.

Commelina

Sometimes known as the Blue Spiderwort, commelina is easy to grow and does best in warm sunny situations. Planting is usually done in the spring and the roots can, if required, be started in pots and planted out of doors towards the end of May. *Commelina tuberosa* produces, in summer, lovely gentian-blue flowers on 15 to 18-in. stems which also carry long lance-shaped leaves.

Convallaria

Although the Lily-of-the-Valley is not a true bulb, it is normally included with bulbous subjects. The best results are secured when the crowns are planted in partial shade and where peat, leafmould and old manure have been added to the soil. Generous treatment will encourage the plants to continue flowering freely over many years and they need only be disturbed and thinned when they become overcrowded. Plant the crowns 3 to 4 in. apart. An annual topdressing of compost or decayed manure applied when the foliage has

Anemone nemorosa

Camassia esculenta

Commelina tuberosa

Convallaria

31

died down will be a great help in the continued production of large bells. Neglected plants produce increasingly small flowers. When picking the flowers, always leave at least one leaf since this foliage is vital if the following year's flowers are to develop.

Lily-of-the-Valley will respond well to forcing when planted into pots or boxes. Retarded crowns are sometimes available and they can be had in flower within three or four weeks from the time of planting and are particularly valuable for producing blooms at Christmas.

Crinum
Natives of several tropical parts of the world, crinums produce ornamental, evergreen, strap-shaped leaves and umbels of funnel-shaped flowers on sturdy stems. They like a rich, loamy, sandy soil containing peat or leafmould. Since they are only hardy in very favoured districts, they are usually grown in pots like agapanthus. Firm planting is essential, potting up being done in March, although established plants can be left three or four years undisturbed, and will benefit by occasional applications of liquid manure during the summer. A few sprayings of clear water will keep the foliage clean and fresh.

Crinum macowanii has a large bulb, sometimes 7 in. or more in diameter. The stem, growing 2 ft. or so high, is crowned with an umbel of nodding, sweetly scented white and purple flowers. *C. moorei* has well-formed, campanulate, pink flowers and is very suitable for growing against a south or south east wall. *C. powellii*, the most widely grown species, will grow out of doors in a sheltered sunny situation and produces handsome white flowers veined red in August and September, the white stamens showing up well.

Crocus
Although they are not by any means the first of the spring-flowering bulbs, crocuses are nevertheless usually regarded as the heralds of spring and no garden is complete without them. Among the earliest to flower are *Crocus imperati*, with scented violet flowers, and *C. sieberi*, which is a lovely lavender-blue colour. After these come the varieties of *C. biflorus*, most of which have a cream or white ground cover with blue or purple feathering.

Crocus ancyrensis (Golden Bunch) has orange-yellow flowers while *C. chrysanthus* has several first-rate varieties including Blue Pearl, pale blue; Snow Bunting, white, feathered purple; and Cream Beauty, ivory white. *C. susianus*, Cloth of Gold Crocus, is a gem for the rock garden, while the silvery-lavender *C. tomasinianus* looks well in a border or in grass. Plant all 3 in. deep.

The large-flowered Dutch crocuses produce a beautiful display in the early spring whether in the rock garden or in the front of beds or borders. Many of them are excellent for naturalising. For bedding they should be planted 3 in. deep fairly closely to obtain maximum results. In the garden they can be left undisturbed for three or four years, while in grassland or woodland they need never be moved and will increase naturally.

Good varieties include Kathleen Parlow, snowy white; Paulus Potter, glossy ruby purple; Yellow Giant, golden yellow; *purpureus grandiflorus*, deep purple; Queen of the Blues, light blue; and Striped Beauty, white striped lilac. The brightest display with crocuses is achieved by planting a mixture of named varieties.

Crocuses are usually regarded as spring-flowering corms, but the large group of autumn crocuses, though similar, are notably hardy and if left undisturbed increase readily from self-sown seed and cormlets. Small patches in borders, rock gardens, shrubberies, woodland, or in grass soon spread into a colony of glorious bloom.

Autumn crocuses grow in any well-drained soil and should be planted 3 in. deep and 2 to 3 in. apart in late July and August for best results. They do well in window-boxes or in pans or trays in the cold greenhouse.

Mixed autumn-flowering species are excellent for gardeners who want a really good show in naturalised conditions. For a continuous long flowering period choose from among the named species. Many flower soon after being planted and before producing foliage.

Among the first to bloom in September is *C. zonatus*, producing large but dainty pinkish-mauve flowers with a gold base and orange-gold anthers. Its leaves appear after the flowers. *C. speciosus* bursts into bloom with bright blue goblets having violet veinings and orange stigmas. The pure white form, *albus*, has a red stigma. This free-flowering gem blooms from late September into October and is particularly delightful when planted with *C. pulchellus*, which has sky-blue flowers and white anthers.

Specialist nurserymen offer other species, and autumn-flowering crocuses are inexpensive. Choose them for colour and flowering time and do naturalise a few dozen to create a carpet effect in grass.

Cyclamen
By careful selection of varieties, it is possible to have flowers of hardy cyclamen in bloom from August until the following May. They are well adapted for growing at the foot of a north-facing wall or under the shelter of trees

Crocus speciosus

Cyclamen repandum

Dahlia Border Prince

where they are charmingly effective. They also naturalise well in grass where it is cool and shady, or in the rock garden in a partially shaded place which has good drainage.

The corms are planted from July onwards, the most suitable soil being a mixture of good fibrous loam, well-decayed leafmould and a proportion of old mortar rubble. Most corms should be covered with about 2 to 3 in. of soil and a topdressing of old leafmould will prove beneficial. All varieties produce attractive flowers with fine, deeply reflexed petals.

Among the best autumn-flowering species is *Cyclamen neapolitanum* with rosy-pink flowers in August and September, the leaves developing just before the flowers fade. The variety *album* has white flowers and charming marbled foliage. *C. europaeum* has fragrant rose-red blooms from August to October and silver marbled leaves. *C. africanum* likes a warm situation, the bluish flowers showing during September and October.

Of the winter and early spring-flowering species, *C. coum*, with rounded green leaves, has pinky-red blooms in February and March. There are two forms, *album*, bluish-white with a dark eye, and *roseum*, with pretty rose-coloured blooms. *C. ibericum* also flowers in February and March and has distinctive silver-zoned foliage at the same time as the flowers appear. It has two forms, *roseum*, rose, and *rubrum*, crimson, which often commence to show colour at the end of January.

Cyclamen repandum produces its silver marbled foliage and bright rose-red flowers from the end of March until May and is the latest of the spring-flowering species.

As cyclamen will grow in sun or shade, they are suitable for planting under shrubs and trees providing a ground covering of foliage and a splash of colour in positions which so often remain bare and uninteresting.

Dahlia

These are among the most showy of summer-flowering plants. Unfortunately, they are only half hardy and tubers cannot be planted out of doors until April. It is possible to start them earlier under glass and they can be planted out of doors as soon as there is no risk of severe frosts. After flowering the tubers should be lifted in the autumn and stored in a dry frostproof place until planting the following spring.

Dahlias revel in rich soil and for preference the site should be prepared in the autumn, working in plenty of decayed manure and bonemeal. If the job cannot be done then, work the soil deeply in early spring. Sometimes the tubers are supplied in polythene bags and these may be safely kept until planting time if stored in a frostproof place.

The planting procedure is simple. Plant each tuber 6 in. deep with the growing tip upwards. Allow 3 ft. between the taller varieties and 2½ ft. between the less tall ones. Drive a tall, stout stake into place before you cover the roots.

Start tying the stems to the stakes when they are about 2 ft. tall. To obtain the finest flowers, the buds should be restricted to one per stem, the end bud being retained and the side buds removed. Dahlias are greedy plants and should have at least one good feed of a fertiliser which is low in nitrogen in late July or early August. Use a handful to each plant, making sure not to touch the leaves, and hoe it into the soil carefully. Keep them free from weeds and water frequently. In a hot summer, mulch the plants with leafmould or compost.

Dahlias should always be given sunny positions—they flower less well in shade. The various types of dahlias are excellent for beds and borders and for cutting. The dwarf bedding varieties can be most effective in window-boxes or in tubs or urns on the terrace or roof garden. Dahlias are divided into clearly defined sections ranging in height from 6 or 7 ft. down to 10 in. These sections also vary in shape, size, and colour of flower. There is a very wide choice of varieties in all the groups.

Eranthis

All Winter Aconites, by which name the eranthis are best known, are dwarf-growing, tuberous-rooted perennials, each crown producing yellow flowers with from five to eight petals. The most popular variety is *Eranthis hyemalis* which has irregularly lobed leaves and bright, glistening golden-yellow flowers resting on emerald-green leaves. *E. cilicica* is very similar but has more divided leaves with a bronzy tinge. *E. tubergeniana* has handsome deep yellow scented flowers, measuring 2 in. across, and its variety Guinea Gold which is somewhat later flowering has deep yellow, fragrant flowers and bronzy foliage.

All varieties do excellently under trees and shrubs where little else will grow and in moist places. When established they provide an attractive green ground covering. Plant the tubers 2 in. deep in autumn or early winter and leave them to naturalise where the soil is fairly well drained.

Eremurus

With their strap-like leaves and long tail-like flower spikes from which they derive their common name, Foxtail Lilies are ideal subjects for the back of the flower border or shrubbery. They look remarkably well planted in groups, the best effect being produced when they are grown among other plants and

Dahlia Daydream

Eremurus himalaicus

Eranthis hyemalis

shrubs. They do, however, need shelter from strong winds.

Before planting, the soil should be deeply cultivated and rotted manure incorporated about 15 in. down. The crowns should be planted during the period October to December and in severe winter weather, a light covering of straw or bracken is advised. They may be left in their flowering quarters for three or four years before lifting and dividing.

Eremurus bungei has spikes of golden-yellow flowers during July and is 5 to 6 ft. high. *E. himalaicus* produces its stately spirals of white flowers with orange anthers during May and June and frequently grows up to 8 ft. tall. *E. robustus elwesianus*, which grows up to 10 ft. tall, carries effective spikes of large delicate pink flowers in June. These are just three of several lovely species and varieties.

Erythronium

Erythroniums are commonly called Dog's Tooth Violets because of the likeness of the little tubers to the teeth of a dog. Early spring flowering, they like a gritty soil and one containing leafmould, peat or old manure. Shady places suit them and they will grow in damp, but not wet, positions. They should be planted 4 to 6 in. deep or a little deeper where

the soil is light. Once in the ground they need not be disturbed for some years for they will multiply quickly.

The leaves of most varieties are prettily splashed with light and dark markings and the nodding blooms are often produced singly, with occasionally two or three per stem. Of the species, *Erythronium albidum* is creamy white. *E. americanum* has golden-yellow flowers on 18-in. stems and, contrary to the others, thrives in full sun, while *E. hendersonii* produces beautiful lavender-pink blooms with maroon centres in March and April on 6-in. branching flower stems.

Other reliable species on 9-in. stems include *E. grandiflorum*, rich yellow with prominent red stamens; *E. revolutum* with large pinkish-purple flowers and its varieties *albiflorum*, creamy white, and Pink Beauty, a real gem. The European Dog's Tooth Violet, *E. dens-canis*, has a number of forms varying in height from 4 to 6 in. flowering in March and April. When established, a mixture of these erythroniums will give an unusual and pleasing display in the front of the border, the rock garden or in grass and among shrubs.

Freesia

Although usually regarded as a greenhouse subject, there is now a strain of freesias

Fritillaria imperialis

available which is quite suitable for growing out of doors. They can be cultivated in exactly the same way as gladioli. The corms should be planted 2 to 3 in. deep from mid-April onwards in a well-drained soil where the situation is not exposed to cutting winds. The colour range is extremely wide. They flower from August onwards but the corms cannot be kept for the following year.

Fritillaria
Fritillaria meleagris, the Snake's Head Fritillary, is a native of Britain and it may still be found growing wild in some districts. It is suitable for growing under trees or naturalising in grass and it will considerably brighten up dull places. A mixture of *F. meleagris* provides an effective show varying in height from 9 to 12 in. Separate varieties are sometimes available including a dark claret purple which is prettily mottled, and *alba* which is pure white, while there are a number of purple and rose varieties. Less common is the variety *contorta* with white blooms on 4-in. stems which are mottled an unusual bronzy shade. *F. citrina* has graceful flowers of pale lemon yellow with bronze shading.

Fritillaria imperialis is the Crown Imperial. It has attractive shiny green leaves, the drooping large bell-shaped flowers appearing at the top of the 3 to $3\frac{1}{2}$-ft. stems, surmounted by a tuft of green foliage. Attractive colours are available including coppery red and yellow, while Orange Brilliant is a handsome variety with large, orange-buff flowers. Aurora, at 4 ft., produces flowers with petals which are orange outside with a golden-yellow interior, at the end of March and during April.

Galanthus
Better known as the very popular snowdrop, galanthus look better planted in groups or drifts rather than in straight rows. For the best results the bulbs should be planted from September to November not less than 4 in. deep, preferably in a well-drained position where they can be left to become established.

Galanthus nivalis is the well-known single snowdrop which is often used for naturalising in grass and shrubberies. The blooms which appear over a long period from January to March have a green mark on the petal edges. The double snowdrop, *G. nivalis flore-pleno*, has a number of very large named varieties.

Galtonia
Often known as the Summer-flowering Hyacinth, this bulb produces long strap-shaped pointed leaves and erect flowering

spikes 4 ft. or more high. These spikes bear twenty or more large, drooping, sweet-scented, pure white bells of great beauty. Planted up to 5 in. deep in the early part of the year, they produce a bold effect the same summer. Left to establish themselves they give a creditable display for many years. *Galtonia candicans* looks well when planted in groups, particularly when placed towards the back of the border or among shrubs.

Gladiolus

It is necessary to lift the corms of gladioli every year and store them dry for the winter as they are slightly tender. The early-flowering or nanus varieties may only be grown in a frostproof greenhouse unless they are planted out in very mild districts and these are dealt with in chapter 10.

The summer-flowering gladioli may be divided into four distinct groups. First come the large-flowered types which flower from July into September and reach a height of up to 4 ft. There are a great many varieties in a wide range of colours. The butterfly gladioli flower at the same time and reach a similar height as the large-flowered types. However, the flowers are smaller and they have distinctive attractive throat markings and blotches, giving the appearance of exotic butterflies.

Miniature gladioli are shorter, about 2 to $2\frac{1}{2}$ ft. tall, often with crinkled edges to the flowers which add to their charm. Primulinus gladioli are 2 to 4 ft. high with more or less hooded flowers set more widely in a slender spike.

Summer-flowering gladioli look lovely in any position and they are ideal for growing in clumps in the border or among shrubs. If they are needed for cutting, they are best planted in the kitchen garden. They give good results when planted in fairly sheltered positions and where they are not exposed to strong winds.

Early soil preparation is advisable so that it is well settled before planting. Plant the corms 4 in. deep from March onwards, the exact time depending on the district, soil and weather conditions. Allow 5 to 6 in. between the corms and except where required entirely for cutting, when they should be planted in rows, clumps or groups of three or more are most effective. A little sand or old ashes placed above and below the corms will keep them from rotting.

A feed in June or July of a good compound fertiliser will often prove beneficial. While the miniature and primulinus gladioli may not need staking, support may be needed by the taller varieties. Exhibitors always stake in order to ensure that the flower stems develop in a really upright position.

After gladioli have flowered and their foliage has died down, they should be lifted and the new developing corms stored in a dry frostproof place until the following spring.

Hyacinthus

Sometimes known as the Queen of Bulbs, the bright and cheerful colours of the hyacinth make it a valuable subject for early bedding and nothing adds more to the attractiveness of the spring garden than a fine display of such fragrant beauty. Rather more expensive than most other bulbs for bedding, they can be interplanted with low-growing plants such as aubrietas, dwarf forget-me-nots, or early flowering pansies which will not only economise on the number of bulbs to be used but produce a charming effect. In addition, the foliage of the other plants will prevent the hyacinth blooms from becoming splashed with soil.

Hyacinths like a well-drained soil in any open sunny position, preferably where the ground has been well dug and enriched with manure, although where this is not available bonemeal may be used. Plant from September to early December and cover them with about 3 in. of soil. A little sand around the bulbs will ensure the best results.

Faded flowers should be removed before the seed pods form; the leaves should not be cut off but allowed to wither. The bulbs will then ripen naturally and flower again the following year, especially if when the foliage has died down, the bulbs are lifted, dried and spread out in trays in any airy place where they can be stored until next planting time.

Among the bedding hyacinths the following are first class in every way and may be depended upon to give a good show. Princess Margaret, light pink; La Victoire, large, red; L'Innocence, white; Bismarck, sky blue; King of Blues, dark blue; and City of Haarlem, yellow.

Iris

There is probably no genus of flowers with such a wide variation of habit and extended colour range as that of the iris. It is not very difficult to obtain a colourful display for at least nine months of the year.

Dutch irises are strong growing with large flowers of great substance, blooming from the end of May onwards. They provide fine colour for the border and are also of great value for forcing, the varieties Wedgwood and Imperator being particularly suited for this purpose. The former grows about 2 ft. and has Wedgwood-blue standards with deeper blue falls. Valuable as a cut flower, Imperator has large lavender-purple standards and broad azure-blue falls with a bril-

Galanthus nivalis

Galtonia candicans

Iris histrioides major

Leucojum vernum

Iris Imperator

Flos Florium – a large-flowered gladiolus

liant yellow blotch. There are many more excellent varieties.

Spanish irises flower about the second week in June and there are many varieties. If the flower spikes are cut when in bud they will open and last a long time in water. Particularly good varieties include Bronze Queen; Cajanus, large canary yellow with orange blotch; La Nuit, dark violet standards and cobalt-blue falls with a yellow blotch; L'Unique, a really handsome flower with a violet-blue standard and a white fall which has a golden blotch. Thunderbolt, or The Great Bronze Iris, produces stately bronze flowers with large orange blotches.

Both Dutch and Spanish irises should be planted about 3 in. deep during September and October and they like an open sunny position with a lightish well-drained soil in which they will multiply rapidly and bloom freely, especially if the soil is given a dressing of bonemeal in the late autumn.

English irises grow 18 to 24 in. high and flower into July. The bulbs should be planted from October onwards. Cover with 3 in. of soil and provide a position which is moist, but by no means waterlogged.

Good varieties of English irises are Baron Von Humboldt, rosy lilac splashed and flaked ruby; King of the Blues; Mont Blanc, pure white; Princess Juliana, deep blue with yellow blotch; and Rosa Bonheur, white flaked rosy purple.

Where the soil is on the dry side, the Spanish and Dutch irises always thrive, while in heavier positions, the English varieties provide a charming display.

Few iris species equal the beauty and attractiveness of *Iris reticulata* which produces its colourful blooms in the dark days of February. Although very charming, it easily establishes itself and may be left in position for five or six years before the bulbs are lifted and divided. It has thin pointed foliage and the scented flowers are a deep purple-violet each with a prominent yellow blotch on 9-in. stems. There are a number of excellent forms including Cantab with delicate blue standards and pale violet-blue falls with a good crest; Royal Blue, a large-flowered, sweet-scented Oxford blue with a yellow blotch; Wentworth, purple-blue; and Hercules, bronze violet.

A position sheltered from strong winds should be selected, for these are liable to damage the early flowers and foliage. Good drainage is important for too much moisture at the roots will soon lead to disease. Groups of six or more give a much more pleasing effect than straight line planting. *Iris danfordiae* is very like *reticulata* in shape but it is pure yellow and shows its flowers on 3-in. stems in February. *I. histrioides major* has blue flowers from January to March.

Muscari armeniacum

Ixia

The African Corn Lilies are very free flowering, producing long graceful racemes of blooms in a wide range of brilliant colours on strong, wiry 16 to 18-in. stems. Flowering out of doors in June–July, each stem carries six or more flowers of striking beauty, most having a prominent dark centre. The narrow grassy foliage is an added attraction and it complements the flowers.

There is a beautiful mixture available in shades of yellow, orange, pink, red and purple. Plant out of doors about the end of October or November, 3 in. deep and 3 in. apart in a sandy loam and in a sunny position where they can be left undisturbed. In cold winters provide a cover of straw or bracken to protect the top growth.

For late spring or early-summer flowering, plant ixias between September and November, five to seven corms to a 6-in. pot in a mixture of sand, leafmould and good garden soil. The pots should then be buried to their rims in peat or ashes in a frame or in the shelter of a wall and protected from frost by glass or straw. In February, when the shoots appear, they can be brought into a cool greenhouse and placed on a sunny shelf. They like a fresh, cool atmosphere and should be kept moist by regular watering.

Ixiolirion

This dainty subject flowers from the end of May onwards producing on thin, stiff 12 to 16-in. tall stems, a number of handsome, rich, violet-blue tubular flowers, in form much like open hyacinth flowers.

Ixiolirions like warm, sheltered positions and rich well-drained sandy soils. Plant 3 in. deep and 3 to 4 in. apart in October where they can be left undisturbed. Like ixia, they appreciate protective covering in the winter. They make the most elegant cut flowers—showy and long lasting.

Of the few species available, *Ixiolirion pallasii* is the most outstanding. It produces lovely large flowers of violet-blue tinged with rose, with a darker coloured band down the centre of each segment. They flower profusely out of doors from the end of May. For cultivation in the cool greenhouse, grow them just as you would ixias.

Leucojum

The leucojums or Snowflakes are of easy culture, thriving in good, moist yet well-drained sandy soil. The smaller varieties are ideal in little groups in the rock garden or in the front of the border but they are really seen at their best in grass or among some dwarf-growing carpeting subject.

Leucojum aestivum, best known as the Summer Snowflake, is probably the widest grown of all the species. Sometimes to be found growing wild in this country, it forms a handsome plant with 18-in. flower spikes in April and May. The elegant, drooping white flowers which have green tips are about 1 in. long and are greatly prized for cutting. Of the same height and blooming at the same time is the variety Gravetye, a greatly improved form, which is larger and more refined than the type.

Leucojum vernum, the Spring Snowflake, is probably the finest of all and is to be found naturalised in some parts of the country. It grows about 6 in. high and for this reason is sometimes mistaken for a snowdrop, although there is a considerable difference in appearance. The sweet-scented flowers of this leucojum are more open and of better shape, each pointed petal being tipped with green making it most attractive. True to its name, it flowers in February and March, although blooms can sometimes be found on established clumps in late January.

Leucojum autumnale, growing 8 in. tall, is not so hardy as those previously mentioned and needs to be planted in very favourable positions. The bulbs are small, and the very thin leaves do not develop until the white, five-petalled flowers, which are lightly tinted pink, are passing over in August.

Lilium

Few flowers surpass lilies for sheer beauty. New varieties and hybrids are constantly being introduced and during recent years there have been improvements in vigour, ease of culture, resistance to disease, plus a tendency for the bulbs to increase more rapidly. Lilies are much easier to grow than is often supposed and none are really expensive considering the magnificent display they give.

Many lilies thrive in the sun, but an even greater number prefer partial shade and are therefore very much at home growing in the herbaceous border or among shrubs, where the lower parts of the stems are shaded. With all lilies, good drainage is important, so everything possible should be done to plant in an open, porous soil, thus avoiding water collecting around the bulbs and encouraging decay. Where the ground is naturally very heavy, it is not difficult to improve it for lilies by removing the existing soil and replacing it with good material. In any case, it is a wise plan, especially with the rather more fastidious varieties, to take out a hole and place a layer of stones or other drainage material at the bottom before returning the soil. Add plenty of leafmould and sand to give porosity, and the bulbs can actually be set in a little envelope of sand.

The depth at which to plant is important and this is determined by the group into which the species falls. Lilies are divided into two groups—those which have only the normal basal roots and those which, in addition, develop secondary roots on the stems. These stem roots die away with the stem.

Generally speaking, non-stem-rooting lilies should be planted at two and a half times the depth of the bulb, with the exception of *Lilium candidum* and *L. giganteum* which should only just be covered. Stem-rooting varieties, on the other hand, must be planted at least 5 in. deep. With these sorts the basal roots feed the developing bulb, but the stem roots, which are abundant, maintain the actual flowers. It is, therefore, most important to know whether the particular variety of lily is a stem rooter or not and plant accordingly.

Which are the best lilies? This is not an easy question to answer because of the immense range of varieties available, but here is a short list of some of the most rewarding species and varieties which can be grown in the ordinary garden.

Lilium auratum is known as the Golden-rayed Lily of Japan. This is stem rooting and produces many highly scented white flowers with crimson spots, each petal marked with a golden ray, on 5 to 7-ft. stems during August and September. Bright Star is an Aurelian hybrid, producing fragrant ivory-white flowers which are apricot inside on 3 to 4-ft. stems in July. It is also stem rooting.

One of the oldest of the cultivated lilies is the Madonna Lily, *L. candidum*, which produces pure white chalice-like flowers on 3 to 4-ft. stems in June and July. Planting time is from early September to October only and the bulbs should be planted shallowly, 1 in. being deep enough.

The Fiesta hybrids have reflexed flowers in yellow, orange or red, all with maroon-black spots, and are 3 to 5 ft. high. Fire King has large brilliant orange-red flowers which are spotted purple and is 2 to 3 ft. high. Golden Splendour has trumpet-shaped flowers of golden yellow with maroon stripes on the reverse of the petals, and is 4 to 6 ft. high.

Lilium hansonii is a bright golden yellow, spotted brown. The fragrant Turk's cap flowers are borne on stems $3\frac{1}{2}$ to 4 ft. high. *L. henryi* has rich deep orange-yellow scented nodding flowers. It is stem rooting and is 5 to 6 ft.

Lilium umbellatum (hollandicum) is the group name of many easily grown stem-rooting hybrids, all flowering in late June. Among the best of these hybrids are Apricot, orange, $1\frac{1}{2}$ ft.; Orange Triumph, many bell-shaped flowers of orange-yellow, 3 ft.; and Vermilion Brilliant, an intense red, $1\frac{1}{2}$ ft.

Montbretia

Lilium auratum

Ixias

43

Lilium lancifolium (*speciosum*) thrives in sun or partial shade and flowers in August or September on 3 to 5-ft. stems. These stem-rooting lilies should be planted about 5 in. deep. *Roseum* is white, heavily spotted pink; *rubrum*, white spotted red; and *album* is pure glistening white.

Lilium longiflorum is an old favourite with lovely trumpet-shaped waxy-white flowers on 3-ft. stems in June and July. *L. martagon* is the true Turk's Cap Lily which will grow in almost any soil or position. Growing 3 to 4 ft. high, the stems produce twenty or more spotted flowers varying from light purple to pale pink. The variety *album* has pure white flowers.

Lilium pardalinum giganteum has large recurved orange-red flowers, spotted purple, and is 5 to 6 ft. high. *L. regale* has fragrant white trumpets with golden-yellow shaded throats, the reverse of the petals being marked brownish-red. It is 3 to 4 ft. high. *L. tenuifolium* has brilliant vivid scarlet Turk's cap flowers on 1 to 2-ft. stems.

Lilium tigrinum splendens, the Tiger Lily, has fiery-orange flowers which are spotted black on 4 to 5-ft. stems. The Mid Century hybrids are a marvellous group of inexpensive stem-rooting lilies derived from *L. tigrinum*. The colours vary from lemon yellow through shades of orange to crimson on 2 to 3-ft. stems. Plant at 5 in. deep. The Olympic hybrids have large trumpets varying from icy green to pink. They are very strong growing reaching a height of 4 to 5 ft.

Lilium bulbs should never be exposed to the light, otherwise the scales will become soft and flabby. If they cannot be planted immediately on receipt, they should be kept in peat or similar material so that they remain firm.

Montbretia

Of South African origin, these produce small graceful arching spikes of bloom. Each corm produces from July to September up to three spikes of tubular flowers in yellow, orange, copper and red combinations. Best planted in groups in the mixed border, they are ideal for cutting. Emily McKenzie is remarkable for its florets which are at least $2\frac{1}{2}$ in. in diameter, the colour being golden orange marked chestnut scarlet. The large-flowered mixed montbretias are well worth growing, as are the Earlham Hybrids.

All montbretias like a deep well-drained loamy soil to which leafmould has been added. Plant the corms 2 to 3 in. deep in sheltered positions in the autumn, or elsewhere in the early spring. Except in cold wet soil, it is not essential to lift the corms annually but do provide a protective covering.

Muscari

The Grape Hyacinths or muscari are easy to grow, flourishing in well-cultivated soil, preferably one enriched with old manure or compost. Ideal for edgings to the flower border and the rock garden, they normally increase fairly quickly by the offsets which form at the base and side of the bulbs. Some varieties can be grown in pots or pans in the cold greenhouse and are suitable for forcing.

Muscari armeniacum Heavenly Blue is one of the best. Flowering in April, it bears 8-in. spikes of fragrant bright gentian blue which are useful for cutting. A newer form is *M. armeniacum* Cantab with clear Cambridge-blue blooms on sturdy stems 6 in. high. *M. azureum* produces 6-in. spikes of bright blue flowers from the end of February. *M. botryoides caeruleum*, or the Italian Grape Hyacinth, bears pretty 6-in. spikes of dark blue, bell-shaped flowers from the end of March, while *M. botryoides album*, white, is an excellent contrast.

Narcissus

Whether grown in pots or borders, naturalised in grass, or as underplanting in the shrubbery, narcissi provide colour and beauty early in the year and by careful selection of varieties one can have a show of bloom from March to May. If left undisturbed they soon become established and flower freely for many years without much attention. For many people they signify spring and as such are a very welcome sight. The popularity of this genus began during the latter half of the last century when a group of enthusiastic growers started cross-breeding until today a marvellous range exists.

The family is divided into a number of groups, most of which are decided by the size of the flowers. Sometimes doubt arises when daffodils are referred to as narcissi. This is quite correct since daffodils with their large trumpets are simply one section of the genus *Narcissus*.

Narcissi form roots early in autumn and the end of August is none too soon to start planting. This should be completed before the last week in September if the finest results are to be obtained, but it can be continued until November. Early planting is especially necessary with the Poeticus varieties, for in the case of this group the old roots remain active even while the fresh roots are forming.

Although not fastidious about soil, narcissi appreciate an open and sunny site that has been well cultivated and manured for a previous crop—a position from which early potatoes have been lifted, for instance, will prove most suitable. They should never be planted on freshly manured land, though ideally the soil should contain plenty of

Narcissus cyclamineus Beryl

Narcissus triandrus albus

humus. Alternatively, the soil may be rendered suitable by an application of bonemeal at the rate of 2 oz. per sq. yd. before the bulbs are planted. Being slow in action, the bonemeal provides nourishment gradually over a long period. The site should be well drained, for a waterlogged, sour soil will not produce good flowers.

For the best effect, bulbs should be planted in groups of at least three rather than in a straight line, and a group of twenty or more bulbs of the same variety can present a really marvellous show. Depth of planting is most important, and many cases of 'blindness' can be attributed to the bulbs being placed too near the surface. On average, they should be covered with 4 in. of soil, though small-sized varieties need not be buried deeper than 2 in. In a heavy soil, additional silver sand around the bulbs will be beneficial and discourage any tendency towards basal rot. Annual lifting is unnecessary—the bulbs can be left undisturbed for several years, but if it becomes necessary to move them or they become overcrowded, this should be done after the foliage has died down in July and the bulbs are dormant. They should then be cleaned and replanted as soon as possible.

When planting, a trowel is greatly preferable to a dibber which is liable to leave a hollow space under the bulb. It is essential that the bulbs be handled carefully when either lifting or planting as any bruising or damage will make it easy for disease or pests to enter. Before replanting, rub off the old, dried and broken bulb tunics, and remove the withered roots, but do not break away any offsets.

It is as well to be clear about the types of bulb offered in catalogues. A mother bulb is one composed of three or more portions, which will normally produce several blooms and can often be divided, if this is very carefully done. A double-nosed bulb has two, often three, flowering 'noses' enclosed in one outer skin. A round bulb has no offsets and is a satisfactory size for planting.

There is a great variation in size and form of narcissi, which include the trumpet varieties usually referred to as daffodils. The following are some reliable varieties.

Trumpet varieties: Beersheba, large pure white; Golden Harvest, very large golden yellow; King Alfred, sometimes known as the aristocrat of daffodils, large golden flower, with the trumpet frilled at the edge; Flower Carpet, another first-class all-yellow variety; Mrs R. O. Backhouse, creamy-white petals, long narrow pearly-pink trumpet.

Large-cupped narcissi varieties: Carlton, clear soft yellow; Carbineer, yellow with

A Large-cupped narcissus

Narcissus February Gold

orange cup; Fortune, bright yellow, deep orange cup; Flower Record, white with yellow cup; Sempre Avanti, creamy white with deep orange cup.

Of the Tazetta (Poetaz) varieties Geranium is most reliable, having several flowers on a stem, each with pure white petals and a geranium-red cup. The Poeticus narcissi have pure white petals and short, flat, brightly coloured cups or crowns. Of these Recurvus or Pheasant's Eye is the best known and valued both for garden use and for cutting. Actaea has a yellow eye edged with scarlet. Jonquils are always popular not only because of the daintiness of their golden-yellow flowers but because of their delightful fragrance.

Apart from the larger, taller growing narcissi and daffodils there are a number of smaller species and varieties which are invaluable for brightening the rock garden, cheering up terraces and window-boxes and contributing to the show in an alpine house. They are also ideal for naturalising, flowering as they do from early March onwards.

Among the choicest of these are the following species growing from 2 to 7 in. high: *Narcissus bulbocodium conspicuus*, Yellow Hoop Petticoat, rich golden-yellow flowers, rush-like foliage, 6 in.; *N. canaliculatus*, three or four scented white flowers with golden-

yellow cup, 6 in.; *N. minimus*, the smallest trumpet narcissus, golden yellow, 2 to 3 in.; *N. nanus*, clear yellow trumpet, 4 in.; *N. triandrus albus*, Angel's Tears, multi-flowering, silvery white, 7 in. Species growing from 8 to 12 in. high include *N. campernelli* (*odorus*), single or double multi-flowering golden-yellow flowers similar to those of the jonquil, scented, 9 to 10 in.; *N. jonquilla*, single, golden-yellow, fragrant flowers, 12 in.; *N. cyclamineus* February Gold, yellow trumpet reflexed petals, 12 in.; *N.* W. P. Milner, sulphur-white trumpet, 8 in.

Species growing 14 to 15 in. high: *N. cyclamineus* Peeping Tom, long, rich golden yellow trumpet, 15 in.; *N. jonquilla* Golden Perfection, golden-yellow flowers, 15 in.; *N. jonquilla* Trevithian, grapefruit-yellow flowers, free flowering and sweetly scented, 15-in. stems; *N. triandrus* Thalia, pure white clusters of flowers, 14 in.

All these miniatures should be planted from late August to the end of October. They can be placed in sun or partial shade in any good garden soil which is well drained. No manure of any kind is needed. About 3 to 4 in. of soil should cover the bulbs, although the smaller miniatures need not be buried quite so deeply. Spacing is a matter of taste, but as narcissi are prolific, increasing very rapidly, 6 to 10 in. apart is a good guide.

Ornithogalum umbellatum

Oxalis adenophylla

Ornithogalum

In the fairly large genus of bulbous plants known as ornithogalums, there are many varieties suitable for the border or rock garden and for cutting. Most are hardy but a few need the protection of a greenhouse.

Any good, well-drained soil will suit the bulbs, which are seen at their best when planted in bold groups. Plant the hardy varieties from September to November, and with some of the choicer kinds, a light top-dressing of decayed manure or peat applied in the early part of the year will keep them in good free-flowering condition.

Ornithogalum nutans produces in May and June umbels of silvery-grey flowers, shaded green on the outside, on 6 to 9-in. stems. It is particularly good for growing in grass or under trees, where it will increase freely. *O. umbellatum*, the Star of Bethlehem, freely produces starry white flowers on 10 to 12-in. stems in May. It increases rapidly but if the clumps are lifted and divided every three years, it proves an effective and attractive subject for the front of the border.

Excellent for growing in the conservatory, but suitable also for growing out of doors in warm, well-drained positions is *O. thyrsoides*, commonly known as the Chincherinchee. This has long, thickish foliage and a dense head of starry white flowers borne on stems 15 in. or more high. It has become very popular during recent years, not only for use in the conservatory and out of doors, but because it makes a first-class cut flower. If cut when the buds are just opening, the flowers will last in water for four or five weeks.

The bulbs should be planted 3 to 4 in. deep from mid-April onwards and this species should be lifted in the autumn before frosts.

Oxalis

The name means sharp or sour, referring to the bitter taste of some of the leaves. Many, but not all, species have tuberous rootstocks. All like congenial conditions and a well-drained soil in a sunny situation.

Oxalis adenophylla is a first-class plant grown in gritty soil in pots or in the rock garden, where its crinkled foliage and rose-pink, semi cup-shaped flowers on 3-in. stems appear from May to July. *O. deppei*, the roots of which are edible, is coppery red and should be divided regularly in October. It never fails to attract attention, whether grown in pots or in the garden. *O. enneaphylla*, white, is absolutely hardy and very attractive, with fan-shaped, much divided leaves and lovely waxy-white flowers. *O. floribunda*, or *rosea*, is the common species with bright pink flowers. It is of very invasive habit and must therefore be kept in its place.

Puschkinia

Puschkinia libanotica, sometimes listed as *P. scilloides*, is better known as the Lebanon or Striped Squill. Growing on 4 to 7-in. stems, the fluffy looking, silvery-blue striped bells appear during March and April in clusters of up to a dozen. Puschkinias are quite hardy and useful for the rock garden, the edge of a border or for woodland areas and, where possible, should be planted in quantity to give the best show. They seem to prefer slightly shady positions where the soil is well drained and on the light side. Plant the bulbs 3 in. deep and about 3 in. apart, preferably where they can be left undisturbed for a number of years.

There is a white form sometimes listed as *P. libanotica alba*, flowering at the same time as the species. Both make a good display if grown in pots or bowls.

Ranunculus

The ranunculus is invaluable for providing an abundance of colourful blooms during May and June. Easy to grow and thriving in almost any situation, it may need some protection from cold winds. Double Turban ranunculus are obtainable in separate colours including scarlet, orange and yellow as well as mixed shades. The Giant French varieties are particularly good for cutting, while the double Persian Mixed strain has many brilliant colours. Tubers should be planted from November to March, claws downwards, 2 in. deep in sandy soil and a light mulching of decayed manure given in early spring will be of great benefit. Ranunculus also make effective pot plants.

Scilla

This genus takes in a very large number of species of varying size. The bulbs produce strap-shaped leaves and spikes bearing six-petalled flowers. Practically all are hardy, although some come from South Africa and other warm places. October is an ideal month to plant and, since the bulbs vary considerably in size, a good guide as to the correct depth for planting is $2\frac{1}{2}$ times the depth of the bulb itself.

Scilla bifolia is a gem for the rock garden, producing bright blue flowers on 4 or 5-in. stems as early as February. It has a white form, *alba*, and a rose-pink variety, *rosea*. *S. sibirica* has vivid Prussian-blue flowers on 4-in. stems and never fails to attract attention, being first class in the front of the border, in the rock garden or grown in pots and pans. The variety *alba* is white, and a remarkable blue form which is rather taller and an improvement on the type is Spring Beauty.

Scilla tubergeniana grows 4 in. high and is most striking; it flowers in February and March, earlier than *S. sibirica*, and is pale blue

Ranunculus

Scilla hispanica rosea

Puschkinia libanotica

in colour with a thin stripe running down the centre of each petal. *S. hispanica* or *campanulata*, often known as the Spanish Bluebell, is altogether larger. It is quite hardy and will thrive in almost any soil. Such varieties as La Grandessa, white, and Myosotis, blue, have been grown for quite a long time, but a number of excellent kinds have recently been introduced which are a great advance on the older types. Flowering in late April and May, they produce really large spikes in choice named varieties. *S. nutans* is our native Bluebell, too well known to need description. It has both white and pink forms, all being excellent for naturalising.

Sparaxis

This small genus of South African origin produces flowers of such brilliant colour combinations that it is often referred to as the Harlequin Flower.

Sparaxis are closely related to ixias although they have larger flowers, averaging 2 in. across, and shorter stems, 6 to 9 in. in height. The narrow foliage is both colourful and graceful. The colour combinations of these soft, delicate flowers are very pleasing and a tremendous asset to the garden from late June into August.

The small globular corms should be planted from the beginning of April onwards, about 3 in. deep and 3 in. apart in light, well-drained soil in sheltered and sunny positions. They like protection in frosty weather.

There are now many beautiful varieties and the most economical and colourful purchase is a mixture. If you want to try a named hybrid, Fire King has flaming red flowers with conspicuous yellow pencillings. These flowers look particularly lovely in the rock garden where they are a delightful addition.

Sternbergia

Sternbergia lutea is an attractive autumn-flowering bulb growing to about 4 to 6 in. in height and producing large, rich golden-yellow blooms in October. It is most effective planted on grassy banks and slopes as well as in the rock garden and borders. If left undisturbed for a long period—it will need a year to become established—it forms large clumps, the brilliance of the flowers contrasting beautifully with the green of the strap-shaped leaves.

The bulbs should be planted in a sunny, well-drained situation in July and covered with 4 to 6 in. of soil. Rooting starts in August and late planting can endanger proper flowering. Dry litter placed over the bulbs during the winter will prevent frost damage. They may also be grown in pots or bowls to flower a few weeks after planting.

Scilla sibirica Spring Beauty

Ornithogalum thrysoides

Darwin tulips

A gay border to welcome the spring

An attractive group of naturalised bulbs

Tigridia

One of the most exotic and unusual of all bulbous flowers for the summer garden is the tigridia, sometimes catalogued as Ferraria and also known as the Peacock Tiger Flower.

The quaint shape and marking of the flowers attract attention wherever they are grown. The blooms are open and shaped rather like a wide, shallow bowl with three broad petals which seem to droop slightly, and three considerably smaller inner petals which are flattened against the bottom of the bowl.

In July and August the 10 to 15-in. stems bear a series of four to six gorgeous flowers which open one after another. Each flower lasts only for a day but a succession is maintained by planting clumps of about two dozen corms. These are inexpensive and make a splendid display because of the brilliant, variable colouring of the flowers, mainly orange-scarlet, spotted with deep crimson at the base of the segments, but there are numerous varieties ranging in colour from white to violet.

Tigridias are as easy to grow as large-flowered gladioli and cultivation is similar. The corms should be planted in late March or April 3 to 4 in. deep and 6 in. apart in rich, well-drained soil. They need warm, sunny positions to thrive and flourish. The soil should be mixed with leafmould and peat before planting with the addition of a little sharp sand placed around each corm. To induce continuous flowering a few applications of liquid manure from the time the first buds appear will be helpful and bring out the real colour tones. When they have finished flowering about the end of August and the foliage has withered lift and store them for the winter in a cool, dry, frostfree place.

Tulipa

For spring bedding there is no flower which has such a wide colour range or which gives such a bright display over so long a period as the tulip. They can be massed in beds by themselves, but the best results are obtained when they are planted with other subjects flowering at the same time such as aubrietas, forget-me-nots, violas or wallflowers. A beautiful effect may be secured with such combinations so long as the correct colour choice is made.

When planting several varieties of tulip together, it is important to use those which will flower at the same time. Early-flowering tulips and Darwins, for instance, planted in the same group will never provide that perfect splash of colour. There is much to be said for planting one variety only in each bed to be certain that the flowers will all show at the

same time, since with different varieties, even of the same class, there is sometimes a few days' difference which may quite spoil the effect.

October and November are suitable months for planting. The beds should be deeply dug and a dressing of well-rotted manure or compost incorporated with the soil, a little bonemeal being a valuable addition. Bury the bulbs at least 4 in. deep, even more in lighter soils, allowing 4 to 6 in. between each bulb to make a really good show.

Single Early tulips can be used for bedding and if given a position which is not bleak or exposed, a brilliant display may often be obtained as early as the end of March. They vary in height from 12 to 14 in. with one or two varieties perhaps an inch taller and are therefore particularly suitable for early bedding. The range of first-class varieties is very wide and among the best are Bellona, pure yellow; Brilliant Star, scarlet; Couleur Cardinal, purplish-crimson; General de Wet, orange; Keizerskroon, scarlet with a yellow edge; and Prince of Austria, orange-red, scented.

Double Early tulips are of great value for beds and borders and also succeed in pots and bowls. The colour range is good, among the best varieties being Electra, cherry red; Maréchal Niel, yellow and orange; Orange Nassau, orange-scarlet; Peach Blossom, rosy pink; and Vuurbaak, scarlet.

Mendel tulips are hybrids between the old Duc van Thol and the Darwins and vary in height from 14 to 24 in. Useful for bedding and forcing, they are available in many attractive varieties including Apricot Beauty, apricot; Athleet, white; Krelage's Triumph, red; Orange Wonder, orange.

Triumph tulips are the result of crossing the Single Earlies with the Darwins, all varieties having stout stems. Alberio is cherry red edged yellow; Elmus, carmine, white edge; Princess Beatrix, scarlet, edged gold; and Rhineland, crimson edged yellow.

Darwin tulips are rather more formal in appearance, producing stems of 24 to 30 in. according to variety. They flower from mid-April onwards. Varieties include Apeldoorn, orange-scarlet; Dover, poppy red; Lefeber's Favourite, glowing scarlet; London, orange-red; and Spring Song, red flushed salmon.

Lily-flowered tulips are May flowering, the petals being pointed and reflexed in a beautiful manner. Good varieties are Aladdin, scarlet edged yellow; Captain Fryatt, garnet red; and Mariette, deep satin rose.

Parrot tulips are quaint and attractive. Flowering from early May onwards most varieties grow 20 to 24 in. high. The flowers, handsomely cut and laciniated, are excellent for cutting. Among the best varieties are Blue

Tulipa greigii

Parrot tulips

Cottage tulips

Zephyranthes candida

Sternbergia lutea

Sparaxis

Parrot, Texas Gold and Fantasy, the latter being an exquisite shade of soft rose with green markings and salmon rose and white on the inside of the flower.

The Cottage or Single Late tulips are hardy, long stemmed and valuable for garden decoration and for cutting. The colour range is extremely wide both in the case of self colours and those of more than one shade and they grow 20 to 26 in. high according to variety. Among the best are Advance, light scarlet; Artist, salmon rose; Mrs John T. Scheepers, yellow; Ossi Oswaldi, creamy white, flushed pink; and Rosy Wings, reddish apricot pink.

The Double Late tulips have been described as peony-flowered tulips since they form very large, full-petalled flowers. Eros is old gold; Nizza, yellow with red spottings; and Orange Triumph, orange-red with yellow edge.

The tulip species or Botanical Tulips provide quite a change from the more usual groups and are available in many different shapes and colours. They grow 4 to 20 in. high and in some of them the wild plant is evident. They flower from February to May according to variety. The three main groups of hybrids can be strongly recommended. These are *Tulipa kaufmanniana*, 4 to 9 in.

with pointed buds and broad, flat flowers; *T. fosteriana*, 8 to 15 in., very large single flowers, suitable for planting in tubs, urns and at the base of trees; and *T. greigii* hybrids, 9 to 20 in., which have very large, bicolor flowers with streaked and mottled foliage. Other individual varieties include *T. eichleri*, vermilion orange and *T. praestans* Fusilier, vermilion.

Zephyranthes

This is known as the Zephyr Flower or Swamp Lily. The bulbs can be grown in light, sandy, well-drained loam in a sunny position, where they produce narrow, strap-shaped leaves and erect, funnel-shaped, crocus-like flowers.

The best known species is *Zephyranthes candida*, with shining white petals and showy, bright yellow anthers. When established it will bloom freely in September and October. *Z. carinata* has large, bright rose flowers in June. In rather open positions a covering of peat or straw during the winter will protect it from frost damage. Similar treatment should be given to *Z. robusta*, the leaves of which appear after the delicate pink flowers in July and August.

Lily-flowered tulips

Tulipa tarda

Peach Blossom—a Double Early tulip

57

Chapter 8   Winter colour in the home

As an inexpensive means of providing colourful floral decorations in the home during the dull weeks of winter and early spring, bulbs are pre-eminent. One does not need to be a skilled gardener or possess special knowledge to grow them successfully, providing a few simple rules are followed carefully. They are easy enough to give even a young child an ideal introduction to the pleasures of gardening.

By growing a selection of suitable kinds and varieties in ornamental bowls and pots of fibre, a showy display can easily be obtained. Such bowls not only lengthen the natural bulb season, but will make welcome gifts for friends at Christmas time and the New Year.

For ornamental bowls without drainage holes, it is essential to use bulb fibre which is readily available. This fibre is light and clean to use, being made up of fibrous peat, crushed oyster shell and a little charcoal to keep it sweet. It must be thoroughly moistened, but not saturated, before use. It is worth remembering that unless they are placed on mats or some other base, earthenware containers are liable to leave damp marks on tables and window-sills.

Fill the bottom of the bowls loosely with fibre, then press it down firmly but not hard. Space the bulbs evenly on top of this and fill in with fibre all around pressing it down well but not too firmly, leaving sufficient space at the top for watering and in the case of hyacinths and narcissi, the tops of the bulbs can be left exposed. Then give a light watering. If the fibre is pressed too firmly, the developing roots of the bulbs will find it difficult to penetrate the hard base and so may push the bulbs upwards.

After planting it is essential to encourage a good root system before the bulbs make too much top growth and this is achieved by placing them in the dark. The ideal method of starting bulbs is to stand the bowls or pots out of doors on a hard base or bed of ashes which does much to prevent worms and soil pests from entering the bowls. Then cover the bowls or pots with 6 in. or so of peat or leafmould and leave them there for eight to ten weeks, looking at them occasionally to make sure the fibre mixture has not dried out. If it has, water as necessary.

This treatment will result in steady growth and a root system able to support good flower spikes. Alternatively, one can simply keep them in a cool dark shed or cellar or even a spare room in the house. In that case, the bowls need examining every week or so to ensure that the fibre is still moist.

After eight to ten weeks the plump white buds will be an inch or so high and they can be brought out into the light so that the leaves will turn green. It is important to accustom the bulbs gradually to both light and heat as a too rapid exposure may cause discoloured leaves or the flower buds may wither.

From this time, regular and copious supplies of water will be necessary according to the temperature of the room in which the bowls are placed. Pour the water in at the side of the bowls, for overhead watering may lead to moisture lodging in the centre of the leaf clusters causing the flower buds to rot off. This is especially so with hyacinths.

Specially prepared bulbs of hyacinths and some narcissi can be grown in glasses of water and there are special vases made for the purpose. They are so manufactured that the bulb rests at the top of the glass and the roots reach down through the narrow neck of the vase. These vases are filled so that the base of the bulb is about $\frac{1}{4}$ in. above the water. It is possible to change the water every three weeks or so but since there is some risk of damaging the roots it is better to place a few lumps of charcoal in the vase at planting time. These lumps, when soaked, remain at the bottom of the vase and will keep the water sweet and check harmful substances from developing. Bulbs grown in water need starting in a cool, dark place for a few weeks so that strong roots develop before they are taken into the living room.

Rules for growing bulbs indoors
1 Use damp fibre in bowls, or sandy soil in pots.
2 Do not make the fibre or soil too solid underneath the bulbs and ensure that the bulbs do not touch each other or the container.
3 Keep them in a cool, dark, airy place for at least eight to ten weeks. Fibre should be

checked regularly as drying out will be detrimental to growth.

4 When the bulbs come indoors, increase the water supply, warmth and light gradually by easy stages. Keep bulbs away from radiators, gas fires and other heating appliances.

5 Wait for the first appearance of the flower bud before standing the bowl or pot in full light—then give plenty of water.

After the bulbs have finished blooming put them in a cool place and water them frequently until the foliage has died down. As soon as the ground is workable in the spring, plant the bulbs out in the garden.

For those who have not the convenience to plant their own bulbs in bowls or do not wish to do so, the pre-planted bulb bowls now available enable them to have the pleasure of growing their own bulbs without effort. For the best results the following simple instructions should be observed.

Gently tip out the contents of the bowl into a larger container; then find the bulbs and place them carefully on one side. Wet the Vermiculite-peat rooting mixture thoroughly with clean tap water, afterwards getting rid of surplus water by gently squeezing it with your hands. Place about two thirds of the moistened mixture back in the bulb bowl and arrange the

Plunging bulbs to encourage the formation of a good root system

Hyacinths may be grown in bowls or specially designed vases

Crocuses on a window-sill

bulbs evenly on it. Place the remainder of the rooting material around and on top of the bulbs, so that their tips are just above the surface.

After planting, store the bowl in a cool, dark and well-aired position, such as a cellar, ventilated cupboard or better still, an unheated shed or some other outside building. In the case of hyacinths, leave them in the cool store until the new shoots are an inch or more high, whilst tulips should be left for at least eight weeks. Inspect the bowl occasionally and water whenever the mixture appears to be drying. If you think too much water has been given, tip the bowl on its side, with one hand over the mixture to prevent it and the bulbs falling out and the surplus will drain off immediately. Do not overwater.

When the new shoots are about 2 in. high, bring the bowls into the light and warmth of a living room, preferably close to a window but not in a cold draught. Water when necessary, but do not give fertiliser or manure of any form.

After flowering do not throw the bulbs away. If you plant them out in the garden, just as they are, leaving the bulbs, roots and rooting mixture intact, they will bloom freely the following spring and for years afterwards.

Bulbs to plant to provide early colour
For Christmas Hippeastrum, hyacinths, *Narcissus* Paper White and Soliel D'or.
January Chionodoxa, crocus species, freesias, galanthus, hyacinths.
February Eranthis, erythronium, *Fritillaria meleagris*, narcissus.
March *Iris reticulata*, muscari, ranunculus, *Scilla sibirica*, tulips.
April Sparaxis, tritonia, tulips.
May Triteleia, ixia, veltheimia.

Gloxinias make attractive house plants

Hyacinths for colour in the early spring

Tulips are very versatile flowering bulbs

Iris reticulata for the home and alpine house

Chapter 9   Greenhouse management

To the modern amateur gardener the greenhouse, home, and garden are no longer separate entities but complementary units. A popular feature of many houses nowadays is the garden room, in which plants play a vital part in the decorative scheme. The greenhouse serves as a supply unit for both garden and house. Not only does it enable the gardener to work in comfort whatever the weather, but it greatly extends the scope of the garden and also prolongs the flowering season.

Although the temperature of a greenhouse may be cold (that is, unheated), cool, intermediate or very warm, a cool greenhouse is the most practical and economical for the amateur. Most bulbous plants will thrive under cool conditions, in which the temperature is maintained between a minimum of 7°C. in winter and 12 to 18°C. in spring and summer.

Heat for the small greenhouse can be provided in a number of ways. Electric heating, though most efficient and easily controlled, can be very expensive to run. Open coal-gas heaters cannot be safely used within the house because the fumes are toxic, but natural (North Sea) gas gives off carbon dioxide which is beneficial to plants. It is now possible to purchase a natural gas heater which is quite safe. Paraffin heating is probably the cheapest method of all, but care must be taken to ensure that the apparatus is kept scrupulously clean, as again, the fumes can cause damage to plants.

It should be remembered, however, that although some artificial heat will be required to maintain minimum temperatures during the winter months, too much at a time when the hours of daylight are short can be disastrous. In the cool house use can be made of sun heat by putting down blinds or shades at night to cut down loss of heat through the glass, provided they are removed promptly to make full use of all available daylight.

The chief difficulty in a small house is to keep the temperatures down in summer, and the ventilators and shades should be operated carefully to avoid big fluctuations or rapid changes of temperature. It may be desirable to use some artificial heat at night when warm, sunny days are followed by cold, sharp nights involving a sudden drop of temperature in the evening.

Ventilators should also be used to control the atmospheric moisture. In a hot, dry spell, humidity must be maintained by damping down floors and staging and spraying the plants themselves frequently. Shading will also be necessary to protect the leaves from the burning rays of the sun and prevent scorching.

When watering the plants, sufficient water should be given at a time to moisten all the soil in the pot. This is best done by watering directly from the spout of the can and not through a rose, a method which also avoids splashing the foliage. It is important to keep the crown of the bulb dry. Experience will soon show when water is required; it can be judged by the weight of the pot or by scratching the surface of the soil with a finger or, in the case of clay pots, by tapping the side to see if it sounds hollow. A more sophisticated watering device is the capillary bench in which the base material of sand or gravel on top of the bench is kept permanently moist and plants receive water through capillary action.

Daffodils may be planted in a double layer which makes for a very attractive display. The bottom of a large bowl should be covered with a layer of compost. Bulbs are evenly spaced on top of this and covered up to their noses in compost. More bulbs are then placed between the noses of the bulbs in the lower layer and covered with compost so that their noses are just showing

It is essential to make sure that all pots are thoroughly clean. The drainage holes must be clear, and crocks should be placed at the bottom of clay pots to assist drainage. This is not essential with plastic pots and pans as the drainage holes are usually adequate. The pot should not be too big for the size of the bulb, or the soil will become sour.

For bulbs planted in pots or pans in the greenhouse, John Innes Potting Compost is a good planting medium, or one of the soilless composts. Other composts are recommended in the descriptive lists. If the bulbs are to be brought into the home for flowering, an ornamental bowl without drainage holes may be preferred, in which case it will be necessary to use special bulb fibre which contains crushed oyster shell and a little charcoal to keep it sweet.

When planting bulbs, the bottom of the pot or bowl is filled with compost or bulb fibre which has been thoroughly moistened. This should be pressed down firmly but not so hard that it will become compacted. The bulbs are laid on the surface of the fibre and when using more than one bulb per pot they should be evenly spaced so that they are not touching one another. The pot is then filled in with compost.

Bulbs can be started into growth either by the method described on page 58 or more usually they can be stood in a cool, dark place such as a cellar or shed, or under the staging in the greenhouse, the object being to encourage them to form a good root system before too much top growth has been made.

Tall plants such as lilies, narcissi and tulips will need staking, and so will those with delicate stems such as freesias. Thin green stakes are best since they are the least obtrusive, and the blooms can be supported by cross-threaded strands of cotton.

All bulbs require a resting period after the foliage dies down, but their individual requirements vary. Instructions are given in the descriptive list that follows.

If good standards of hygiene are maintained in the greenhouse, pests and diseases will be kept to the minimum. A constant watch should be kept and spraying with a good derris-based insecticide carried out when necessary against pests such as aphids. When planting, it is important to examine bulbs carefully and discard those that are damaged or show signs of disease. Infested or infected bulbs should always be burned.

Most cool greenhouse owners follow a three-part programme, the main flowering seasons being spring, summer and autumn. This does not mean a flowerless winter, only that less colour can be expected in the depth of winter.

Many of the smaller bulbs are ideal for growing in the alpine house or cold greenhouse in pans or wide-topped pots. This will lead to a colourful display from January onwards. Not only will such protection encourage earlier, cleaner flowers, but they will be seen from a better and closer angle than when viewed in their normal open-ground positions.

Free ventilation is needed to encourage sturdy growth and to stave off mildew. Practically all bulbs can be grown satisfactorily in the John Innes Potting mixtures using well-crocked pans or pots. Watering needs to be carried out with care and particularly in very cold weather it is best to keep the bulbs on the dry side.

The following plants are very suitable for pans or pots in the alpine house: *Anemone blanda*, crocus species, colchicums, hardy cyclamens, galanthus or snowdrops, *Iris reticulata*, *I. danfordiae*, dwarf narcissi, scillas, and tulip species.

Watering a cyclamen and staking daffodils

Resting hippeastrums under the staging in the greenhouse

Chapter 10 An A-Z guide to bulbs for the greenhouse

Achimenes

These gay, easy-to-grow, long-lasting flowers in pink, purple and white are very popular for pots and hanging baskets inside the greenhouse. The tubers are available in mixture from January until April.

Plant them in a fine mixture of loam, peat, sand and some well-decayed manure. Cover them an inch deep and once top growth appears give plenty of light and regular watering. The tubular flowers appear on 15 to 18-in. stems and should be given some light support unless they are growing in hanging baskets. After flowering they can be stored dry in their pots in a temperature of about 10°C. until it is time to start them into growth again.

Begonia

The tuberous-rooted double begonias are among the most colourful of the family, with bold flowers in vivid shades of yellow, orange and scarlet.

For indoor use, the tubers should be started into growth in February or March in a temperature of not less than 10°C. At the same time, care must be taken not to let the temperature go above 18°C., and it should be kept as even as possible to ensure steady growth without checks.

Trays or shallow boxes should be filled with a mixture of one part each of good sweet loam and leafmould, with a half part of coarse silver sand. See that these are well mixed and moist without being wet. The tubers should then be firmly set in the boxes with their rounded surface downwards, for it is from the dented surface that the new shoots appear. Do not place them too closely, otherwise the fibrous roots will become matted together and broken when the tubers are later transferred to pots. Leave the crowns of the tubers exposed to discourage any tendency to rotting.

The best growth is produced in a humid atmosphere. As soon as the shoots are an inch high, the tubers should be potted up singly in a mixture of well broken-down turf or fibrous loam, leafmould or peat, a little silver sand and, wherever possible some old cow manure. Failing this, well-decayed stable manure or bonemeal should be included.

For the first potting, use the 3½-in. size, except in the case of older tubers, which may be large and therefore need a 5-in. pot. If the potting mixture is brought into the shed or greenhouse the day before use, it will be warmer and therefore will not check the growing tubers so much. Loosen and lift the tubers from the box with great care, so as not to damage the roots, especially the tips. Then, having put some crocks at the bottom of the pot and half filled it with soil, place a tuber on the surface and gently fill in and firm the soil around it, finishing off so that the top of the tuber can just be seen.

Do not subject the newly potted plants to strong light for a few days, but afterwards give plenty of light and air, watering as necessary. It is always wise to avoid watering begonias when the full sun falls on the foliage, for this may lead to spotting.

For outdoor cultivation, the tubers need not be boxed until April. The growing plants are subsequently hardened off before being bedded out. Planting out of doors should not be attempted before the end of May or early June when all danger of frost is past; if the soil is fairly moist then growth will be rapid and flowers will soon appear.

After flowering the tubers should be removed from pots or beds when the foliage has died down, carefully cleaned and stored in a dry, frostproof place until the next planting time. It is wise to examine them occasionally during the winter, and remove any damaged or decayed specimens before they spread disease.

Bletilla

Although many species of this genus, a member of the orchid family, require almost sub-tropical conditions, *Bletilla striata*, sometimes known as *B. hyacinthina*, is comparatively hardy, though it may need the protection of a greenhouse in winter. It forms a tuberous rootstock and thrives best in semi-shady positions. It should be given well-drained loamy soil in which there is plenty of leafmould.

The leaves are hairy and the slender flower stems, varying from 6 to 12 in. high, produce during the summer, four or five nodding rose-purple flowers with narrow petals.

Achimenes

Sam Phillips—a tuberous-rooted begonia

Narcissus bulbocodium for the alpine house

Rose Princess—another showy begonia variety

65

Eucomis punctata

Freesias

Apart from their use out of doors, bletillas are excellent subjects for the cold greenhouse. Water very sparingly in winter, only just enough to keep the soil from becoming bone dry.

Canna
This tall-growing plant owes its name to its erect stems or canes. Although it will not stand frosts, it is a useful plant for summer bedding in sheltered, sunny situations, and looks attractive when intermixed with other summer bedding subjects.

The thickish rootstocks should be started into growth from early February to April, preferably in a temperature of around 15 to 18°C. Cannas like a fairly rich sandy compost and moist growing atmosphere. Although they look first class in the greenhouse, they are at their best out of doors and can be moved to their flowering quarters from early June onwards.

Slugs and snails are the most likely pests. The foliage should be examined at frequent intervals and slug bait can be put down.

Among the first-class named varieties are those with scarlet, orange and yellow, yellow with dark spots, and orange-scarlet flowers, some having attractive purplish-brown foliage which, with the flowers, combines to make an exotic-looking subject.

Clivia
Of South African origin, these plants with their attractive clusters of funnel-shaped flowers on sturdy stems are easy to grow. There are several species, all flourishing in the cool greenhouse or on a window-sill, so long as they are kept free from frost.

Many useful hybrids have been raised. The best known species is *Clivia miniata*, which has several forms and is a native of Natal; the bright green strap-shaped leaves grow from 18 to 24 in. long and the 15 to 18-in. stem is surmounted with an umbel of twelve to eighteen campanulate scarlet flowers, each one having a yellow throat, making an effective display during the winter. *C. nobilis* is not quite so large as *C. miniata* and has orange-red flowers, the petals of which are tipped with green. The flowers of both are scented and sometimes followed by large, brilliant red berries.

A compost of two parts loam, one part decayed manure, plus silver sand and a dusting of charcoal, suits the plants, which like plenty of moisture during their growing period. They should be disturbed only when it is necessary to divide; in fact they seem to flower better when pot-bound. Well-established plants will benefit from a few applications of liquid manure when in full growth.

Cyclamen

Cyclamen persicum is among the showiest of all winter and spring-flowering greenhouse and living-room plants. Even when not in bloom, the modern giant forms are attractive, with their handsome, often silvered foliage. If you have a cool greenhouse from which frost can be excluded, there is no difficulty in growing cyclamen.

Corms can be started into growth from July onwards. Plant them concave side upwards and leave the top exposed. They are best started in $3\frac{1}{2}$-in. pots for this lessens the risk of overwatering. As growth proceeds, move to 5-in. pots, which should be well crocked. The John Innes No. 3 compost is quite suitable, and so are the peat-based composts. After potting, leave the plants in a cold frame, keeping the compost moist and the frame closed until growth starts. Then give more ventilation and keep the pots shaded.

Towards the end of September, bring them into the greenhouse where the temperature remains between 10 and 12°C. Keep the compost moist, giving good soakings when needed rather than daily sprinklings. Bad drainage soon spoils the plants. When removing discoloured foliage and faded flowers, pull out the stems close to the corms, otherwise decay may set in. After flowering, much less moisture is needed, but it is not essential to dry off the corms.

Eucomis

This bulbous plant deserves to be more widely known. It has the common name of Pineapple Flower and makes an excellent pot plant. The wavy leaves, often as much as 18 in. long and 2 or 3 in. wide, are spotted purplish brown on the undersides. At the top of each sturdy 10 to 14-in. spike is a densely packed head surrounded with a little tuft of bracts.

Eucomis bicolor is a vigorous species, the greenish-yellow flowers being edged with purple. *E. punctata* is a fine species, its creamy-yellow, star-shaped flowers appearing from July until September. The pleasing scent is particularly strong.

Eucomis like rich, well-drained gritty soil. In mild districts they can be grown out of doors in a warm, sheltered situation. A winter mulching of leafmould or weathered ashes will provide protection.

Freesia

This South African genus has long been valued as a greenhouse flowering plant, particularly for its grace and fragrance. The colour range is extremely wide, and most flowers are beautifully scented.

Cyclamen persicum

Freesias do best when grown in pots or boxes rather than in bowls and planting should be done from August onwards. With a temperature of 15 to 18°C. it should be possible to have flowers from the end of December onwards. A suitable planting mixture consists of 4 parts loam and 1 part each of silver sand, rotted manure and leafmould, or the John Innes composts can be used.

After planting, stand the pots in a cold frame or sheltered position and water sparingly. When top growth is seen, the plants can be gradually introduced into warmth but too much heat causes blindness. As soon as the flower spikes develop, feeds of liquid manure at ten-day intervals will be helpful.

Canna

Clivia miniata

Freesias can also be raised from seed which, if sown in a temperature of 15 to 18 °C. early in the year, will produce highly scented flowers within six or seven months. Seed should be sown thinly directly into pots or boxes of sandy compost, but the seedlings should not be transplanted since they do not stand this treatment well.

Gladiolus
While it is possible to grow the large-flowered and primulinus types of gladiolus in the greenhouse, the smaller flowering and early species are the best for this purpose. Cultural details for the hardy gladioli are to be found on page 38.

Corms should be planted in pots in November, four or five corms to each 5 or 6-in. pot. They should be kept under cool conditions and will then flower from mid-April onwards. The flowers of all are much daintier than the large-flowered type. Among the best is *Gladiolus colvillei* which has dainty crimson-purple flowers flecked with white. *G. nanus* can also be recommended and of its forms, which grow 1 to 2 ft. high, Amanda May, salmon pink; Blushing Bride, white, flaked crimson; Peach Blossom, pink; and Spitfire, scarlet, are all first class. All are excellent for cutting.

Gloxinia
Tuberous plants with large, bell-shaped flowers in crimson, violet and white marked with other colours, gloxinias are among one of the most decorative greenhouse plants. These should be treated in the same way as begonias, the tubers being started in pots and barely covered, in February and March, with a rich, well-drained compost. If a fertiliser has not been incorporated with the mixture, occasional applications of liquid manure during the growing season will prove beneficial. Avoid much watering until the tubers are in full growth and keep the receptacles shaded, potting on the plants as growth develops.

Gloxinias flower from June until September. It is important to keep the plants scrupulously clean, to minimise pests and diseases.

Haemanthus
Sometimes known as the Blood Flower, this is a greenhouse bulbous plant of South African origin which is easy to cultivate. It should be grown in the cool greenhouse, although in warm positions it will sometimes flourish outside.

The broad, thick, fleshy leaves are produced on 10 to 15-in. high speckled flower stems. Plant the bulbs in September and they will

Lilium Enchantment

Hippeastrum

flower during winter and spring. One bulb in a 5-in. pot of sandy loam will produce a good effect, although several bulbs in a larger container provide the best display. The bulbs resent disturbance and it is unnecessary to repot more than once every three years or so. In such cases remove the top couple of inches of soil, and replace it with fresh material.

Haemanthus albiflos is pure white; *H. coccineus*, bright red speckled with brown and *H. katharinae* is brilliant red.

Hippeastrum
Hippeastrums, now so popular as house plants, can also be grown in the greenhouse with little heat except for an initial burst. Bulbs can be obtained which will produce flowers in pink, red, crimson, orange and white, as well as all these colours striped with white. They like a well-drained soil which is fairly rich in organic matter and succeed when potted one bulb per 6 to 8-in. pot in John Innes Potting Compost No. 3. You can also prepare your own potting mixture of 3 parts good loam to 1 part well-decayed manure, with some silver sand and bonemeal. Good drainage is ensured by placing an inch or so of broken crocks in the bottom of the pot. When potting, a third to a half of the bulb should remain above the soil.

Hippeastrums should be started into growth in the greenhouse from February onwards, preferably in succession until the end of April. After potting, soak the soil, but not the bulb, and place in full light in the greenhouse in a temperature of 15 to 21°C. Bottom heat, i.e. heat given from the staging on which the pot stands, is best. Very little water should be given until the bud starts to show, when normal watering can be resumed. As soon as the buds begin to burst you can allow the temperature in the greenhouse to fall as low as 7°C. to lengthen the flowering period.

Continue to water the plant when it has finished flowering, giving it a feed of liquid manure each time until late August. After the foliage has withered, take the bulb from the pot, let it dry and store it in a warm place before potting it up again the following February for the next season.

Hymenocallis (Ismene)
These greenhouse bulbs are native of tropical America and are often known as Sea Daffodils. The bulbs should be potted in early March, using a mixture of turfy loam, decayed manure and coarse silver sand. Once growth is seen water should be given frequently and the temperature maintained at about 15°C. The bulbs should be partly rested during the

winter by gradually withholding water. It is not necessary to disturb the roots annually; it is sufficient to repot the bulbs once in every three years, for the same bulbs go on flowering for a number of years. *Hymenocallis calathina* and its improved form Advance, with white flowers growing 2 ft. high, are the best for general purposes, while the variety Sulphur Queen has soft creamy-yellow trumpet-shaped blooms.

Ixia

The Corn Lilies, native of South Africa, are very valuable for cool greenhouse cultivation, for they flower in late spring and early summer in abundance and do not require special treatment. The wiry, but strong stems grow 15 to 18 in. tall, each producing six or more flowers of striking beauty with most having a prominent dark centre. The narrow foliage is an added attraction for indoor decoration.

Ixias can be given the same treatment as freesias, except that the pots are best plunged up to their rims in peat and left in a sheltered position or cold frame until February. When brought into the cool greenhouse and placed on a sunny shelf, they will soon produce a fine display. Like freesias, they can be purchased as mixed selections or by named variety.

Lilium

There are a number of lilies which respond well to greenhouse treatment without a lot of heat. Among the best of these is *Lilium auratum* and its forms, and *L. longiflorum* which also has several forms including *giganteum* and *harrisii*, the latter sometimes being known as the Easter Lily. Other good lilies are *L. lancifolium* (*speciosum*) and several of its forms including *rubrum*, *roseum* and *melpomene*. *Lilium regale* is also first class in pots and has the advantage of being heavily scented. It grows 3 to 4 ft. high and the large, white trumpets have a golden band in the centre. Other taller lilies include *L. henryi*, orange-yellow.

Among the newer hybrids the following four varieties are easily grown in 5 or 6-in. pots in an ordinary living room as well as in a cold greenhouse. Keep them under cool conditions until growth is about an inch high. They are also suitable for growing out of doors. Enchantment, 2 to 3 ft. Large, upright flowers of blazing nasturtium red. Vigorous, prolific and outstanding for pots or garden. Harmony, 2 to 3 ft. Large, wide-petalled, upright flowers in rich, brilliant, orange shades. Prosperity, 3 ft. Outward-facing lemon-yellow flowers. Vigorous, increasing quickly. Paprika, 2 to 3 ft. Outward-facing large flowers of deep, rich crimson. Vigorous.

Nerine

These are bulbous plants which give a brilliant display with the minimum of trouble. They do not require much heat; in fact, nerines will flourish so long as frost can be excluded from the greenhouse and they are given plenty of air and sunshine.

The bulbs should be planted in August or early September in $3\frac{1}{2}$ or 4-in. pots according to their size. Use a well-drained soil mixture containing silver sand and bonemeal, while the addition of decayed manure will be helpful. Plant so that just the neck of the bulbs is left exposed and keep the compost moist without being wet.

The blooms develop quickly, appearing in September and October before the foliage is seen. Keep the bulbs supplied with moisture after the flowers are over, for this encourages the development of the foliage on which largely depends the flowering display the following season. About the middle of May the leaves turn yellow and watering should then be gradually reduced and the bulbs allowed to ripen in their pots. Repotting is only necessary every third year.

The majority of nerines produce their umbels of brilliantly coloured flowers on 12 to 18-in. stems. *Nerine sarniensis*, the Guernsey Lily, has pink flowers speckled with gold when seen in the sunlight. *N. flexuosa* has large heads of pale pink flowers, while *N. crispa* (*undulata*) is another first-class pink species. *N. bowdenii* is carmine pink and one of the hardiest varieties, sometimes being planted out of doors in sheltered positions such as at the base of a wall. The florets have tiny golden spots on the petals which glisten in the sun.

Oxalis

These are easy to grow as pot plants in a cool greenhouse. Plant eight or nine bulbs to each 5-in. pot in a compost of sandy loam and leafmould, covering them to a depth of only about $\frac{1}{2}$ in. After potting, keep in a cool place until growth appears and then move to the light. No water should be given until growth appears and then only sparingly, with an occasional application of liquid manure. There are a number of species but the easiest to grow are *Oxalis adenophylla*, 3 in. tall, with dwarf lilac-pink flowers and crinkled foliage, and *O. deppei*, with dainty coppery-red flowers and clover-like leaves marked with bands of purple. *O. adenophylla* flowers from April to June, well ahead of *O. deppei*.

Sparaxis

Sometimes called the Harlequin Flower with richly coloured flowers and colourful foliage on 6-in. stems, sparaxis is easily grown in a

Nerine sarniensis

Hymenocallis calathina

Haemanthus katharinae

A greenhouse with daffodils and cyclamen

Sprekelia formosissima

Tritonia

cool greenhouse. Plant the corms in pots in October and treat them in the same way as ixias. Selections of mixed hybrids are available from nurserymen.

Sprekelia
Sprekelia formosissima, the Jacobean Lily and a native of Mexico, flowers well in pots of sandy loam in the cool greenhouse. The bulbs are 2 in. in diameter and the vivid crimson-scarlet flowers are produced in March and April. These are orchid-like in appearance with six long petals, although growing on 18 to 24-in. stems. The bulbs, two thirds buried, should be potted up in February. Water freely when in full growth.

Tigridia
Natives of Mexico and Peru, these are interesting bulbous plants often known as Tiger Flowers because of their beautifully spotted and marked flowers. They make first-class pot plants and will flower from June onwards. They may also be planted out of doors in summer in sunny positions, and are described in more detail in the chapter on hardy bulbous plants.

There are a number of separately named varieties, but tigridias are usually offered in mixture.

Tritonia
This is a pretty genus flowering in June and July, with leaves about 6 in. long and slender stems growing 12 to 15 in. tall, with orange-shaded flowers shaped like broad, short funnels. Tritonias cannot be grown out of doors except in very mild districts, but can be cultivated in a cool greenhouse in the same way as ixias. Try *crocata rosea* or Orange Delight, a strong long-lasting variety of great beauty.

Tulipa
Apart from their value for growing in bowls in the living room, tulips can be used for increasing the colour display in the greenhouse early in the year. September is a good month to plant. Crock the pots well, then add some leafmould or peat before putting in John Innes Potting Compost No. 2. Work the compost around the bulbs without making it too firm, leaving the very tips of the bulbs just exposed.

Place the pots out of doors on a hard base covering them with at least 2 in. of leafmould, sandy soil or weathered ashes. Leave them for about eight weeks by which time they will have made a good root system and an inch or so of top growth. Bring them into a cool greenhouse and dull light for a week and then stand them in full light in a temperature of 15 to 21°C., watering freely. Once the flower buds expand the temperature can be reduced.

Single Early varieties growing 12 to 15 in. high include Brilliant Star, scarlet; Couleur Cardinal, purplish-crimson; General de Wet, orange; and Prince of Austria, orange-red. Good Double Early varieties are Electra, cherry red; Orange Nassau, orange-scarlet; Peach Blossom, rosy pink; and Vuurbaak, scarlet. A few of the Mendels and Darwins are also successful in the greenhouse. Most interesting of all, however, are the tulip species with their exotic shapes and colourings. These include *Tulipa batalinii*, rich yellow; *T. clusiana*, creamy white and red; *T. fosteriana* Red Emperor and *T. greigii*, of which there are many named hybrids, most of which are beautifully marked red, yellow and bronze, many with mottled foliage. *T. kaufmanniana*, the Water Lily tulip, grows 5 to 7 in. high with creamy-white flowers tinted carmine. It has many choice named hybrids varying in height from 4 to 9 in. high.

Vallota
This plant was once much in favour for growing on the window-sill where it proved of great value for its fine free-flowering abilities. Although often reaching 15 to 18 in. high, *Vallota speciosa* will, on occasion, produce scapes or growing stems up to 3 ft. surmounted with six to nine funnel-shaped, brilliant scarlet flowers. More often, however, the plants are grown in 5-in. diameter pots and produce three or four flowers on 12 to 15-in. stems.

It is not necessary to dry off the bulbs; in fact, part of the plant's charm lies in its evergreen strap-shaped leaves, which are often 18 to 24 in. long. To keep the plants healthy, the bulbs must be liberally supplied with water during their growing period, and the soil kept just moist when the plants are at rest.

Bulbs should be potted from June to September, using a sandy compost containing decayed manure and leafmould. Repotting is not necessary more than once every three years. In alternate seasons, remove the top inch of soil, replacing it with fresh material.

Veltheimia
There are few species of this genus all of which may be successfully grown with very little artificial heat.

The broad leaves with wavy edges are 6 to 8 in. wide and the flower spikes, often 18 to 30 in. high, are not unlike the miniature Red-hot Pokers of the herbaceous border. These leafless spikes often carry thirty to forty or even more individual tubular florets which, in the case of *Veltheimia glauca* are

red and yellow, set off by glaucous foliage, while *V. viridiflora* is deep flesh pink mottled green with bright green leaves.

The bulbs should be potted in August or early September and provided with a compost of good loam, some peat or leafmould and silver sand, with the addition of well-rotted manure. Start the bulbs in a low temperature and when there are signs of growth, heat can be increased.

Zantedeschia
This is the name by which Arum Lilies, so long known as richardia, are to be called now botanists and other scientists have decided that they should be reclassified. Several species are invaluable for greenhouse and church decoration. All are perennial, with thick, fleshy roots and large leaves. The flowering part of the plant consists of an erect, club-like spadix, more or less enclosed by a large, funnel-shaped spathe.

Of the species available, *Zantedeschia rehmannii*, summer flowering, has rose-purple spathes and also forms which are both red and scarlet. *Z. elliottiana*, early summer flowering, is a fine species with pure yellow spathes and dark green foliage, heavily mottled with white. Very similar is *Z. pentlandii*, with golden flowers and large green leaves. *Z. africana*, or *aethiopica*, is the well-known pure white species so much used for decoration.

The cultivation of *Z. aethiopica*, the Common Arum Lily, is as follows. The plants, which have been dried off during the summer, are cleaned at the end of August or early in September and the offsets removed and potted separately. They can be kept out of doors until late September, then transferred under glass and kept at first in a temperature of 10°C., which is afterwards increased to 15°C. Where there is plenty of greenhouse room, the tuberous roots can be planted in beds of fairly rich but not freshly manured compost, or they may be grown in large boxes.

Generally speaking, when space is limited, the roots are potted up. A good sized root will need anything from a 5 to 7-in. diameter pot filled with a fibrous loam, peat, sand and bonemeal (stable manure is best avoided). Three tubers in a large receptacle produce a striking effect. Water only as necessary, and keep the pots in a temperature of around 15°C. giving ventilation whenever the conditions are favourable.

Blooms usually appear from December onwards, but feeding with liquid manure should not be started until February and is often not necessary then, although it may be helpful in producing successive blooms, especially around Easter time.

Zantedeschia elliottiana

Vallota

Veltheimia viridiflora

75

Chapter 11   Pests and diseases

The aim should be to prevent rather than cure pests and diseases and this means that a high standard of cleanliness in garden, frame, greenhouse and storage place must always be maintained. Partly diseased bulbs and bulb remains should always be burned and steps should be taken against slugs, snails and aphids, for often even slight damage by pests opens the way for disease spores.

Occasionally the lower parts of bulbs are damaged by boring pests such as wireworms, and where they are suspected one of the good soil fumigants should be worked into the ground.

Of the larger pests, mice are perhaps the most troublesome both when bulbs are in store and when growing. Traps or one of the baits available on the market are reliable ways of getting rid of them, although the instructions given for the use of the bait should be rigidly followed. This ensures that no harm is done to domestic animals and birds.

In woodland areas, rabbits and hares may eat the young growths and some method must be devised to keep them away. Aphids of various kinds are harmful to growing plants since they suck the sap from the foliage causing the leaves to become twisted, malformed and discoloured. They also transmit virus troubles and the honeydew they secrete encourages ants. A good derris-based insecticide applied at frequent intervals where aphids are seen or suspected should soon eradicate the pests.

If when lifted a bulb is found to be infested, it should be destroyed by burning and apparently healthy bulbs lifted in the same batch should be dipped in a good insecticide.

Narcissus flies can be destructive. There is a type sometimes identified as the merodon or eumerus fly which has a grub-like larva and this burrows into bulbs which then become soft and decay from the base. If leaves develop they are twisted and stunted. Affected plants are best burned although commercial growers have had success in immersing them in water at a temperature of 45°C. since this kills the grubs without harming the bulbs. The same pests also attack some other bulbs.

Stem and bulb eelworms are extremely small and only visible under a microscope.

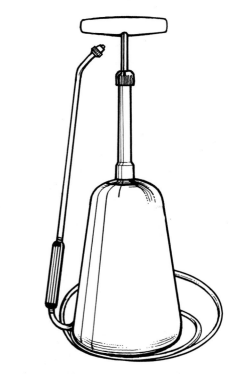

Two different kinds of chemical sprayer

Greenfly

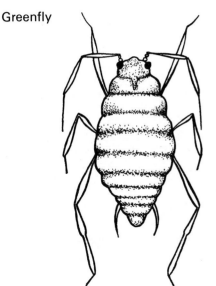

The larvae of the narcissus fly

Tulip fire

They are usually first noticed when the leaves become malformed and sometimes streaked. If a bulb is cut, it will show brown patches or lines. This pest is liable to attack not only narcissi, but tulips, iris and hyacinths. The same treatment is needed as for narcissus fly although most gardeners decide to burn affected bulbs.

Thrips are very minute pests which cause silvery markings on the leaves and often on the flowers. Although gladioli are the most commonly attacked, they will affect various other bulbs such as cyclamen and hippeastrums. If nothing is done to destroy the pests, they will crawl down the stems in the autumn and hide under the dry skins of the new corms and reappear the following season. Many gardeners destroy the growths as soon as the silvery markings are seen. Lindex, or one of the other modern systemic sprays, is effective or a nicotine-based spray can be used. When the corms are stored they should be dusted with whizzed naphthalene which will help to destroy the pests.

There are few diseases which trouble bulbs grown under ordinary good conditions. Botrytis is one of the most serious problems, particularly affecting liliums and tulips. It is generally to be seen as brown spots or markings on the leaves and stems and is more likely to appear in a damp season. It first shows itself as brownish markings which later turn a greyish colour and the leaves drop and the stems may collapse. A simple remedy is to spray the entire batch of plants with Bordeaux Mixture.

Tulips are affected by a related form of botrytis, the disease in this case being referred to as tulip fire. The plants become stunted and the foliage withers and turns greyish brown. It spreads rapidly, particularly in damp weather. Where the disease occurs, it is best not to grow liliums or tulips on the same site for two or three years.

Occasionally bulbs are affected by a basal rot which is a form of fusarium. It is often first noticed when the bulbs are stored and they become soft. Such specimens should not be planted but destroyed.

Occasionally the bulbs of *Iris reticulata* become spotted with ink-like markings. This causes the bulb to rot and all bulbs however slightly affected should be burned since there is no cure.

Virus troubles are only likely to occur when aphids are not dealt with. When they do appear they cause distinct yellow stripes on the foliage and the bulbs become weakened, but it does not mean that every bulb showing foliage with yellow stripes is affected by virus. This may simply be due to local—soil or climatic—conditions.

Index
Figures in italics
indicate an illustration